Copyright © 2017 Dea Bernadette D. Suselo
All rights reserved.

ISBN: 9781726766999

www.facebook.com/DeaBernadette

Period: Ayutthaya

During the war period (The late era of Ayutthaya), many women costumes were designed for wearer in order to move easier. Women wore a cloth that crosses their chest and tied up over their neck.

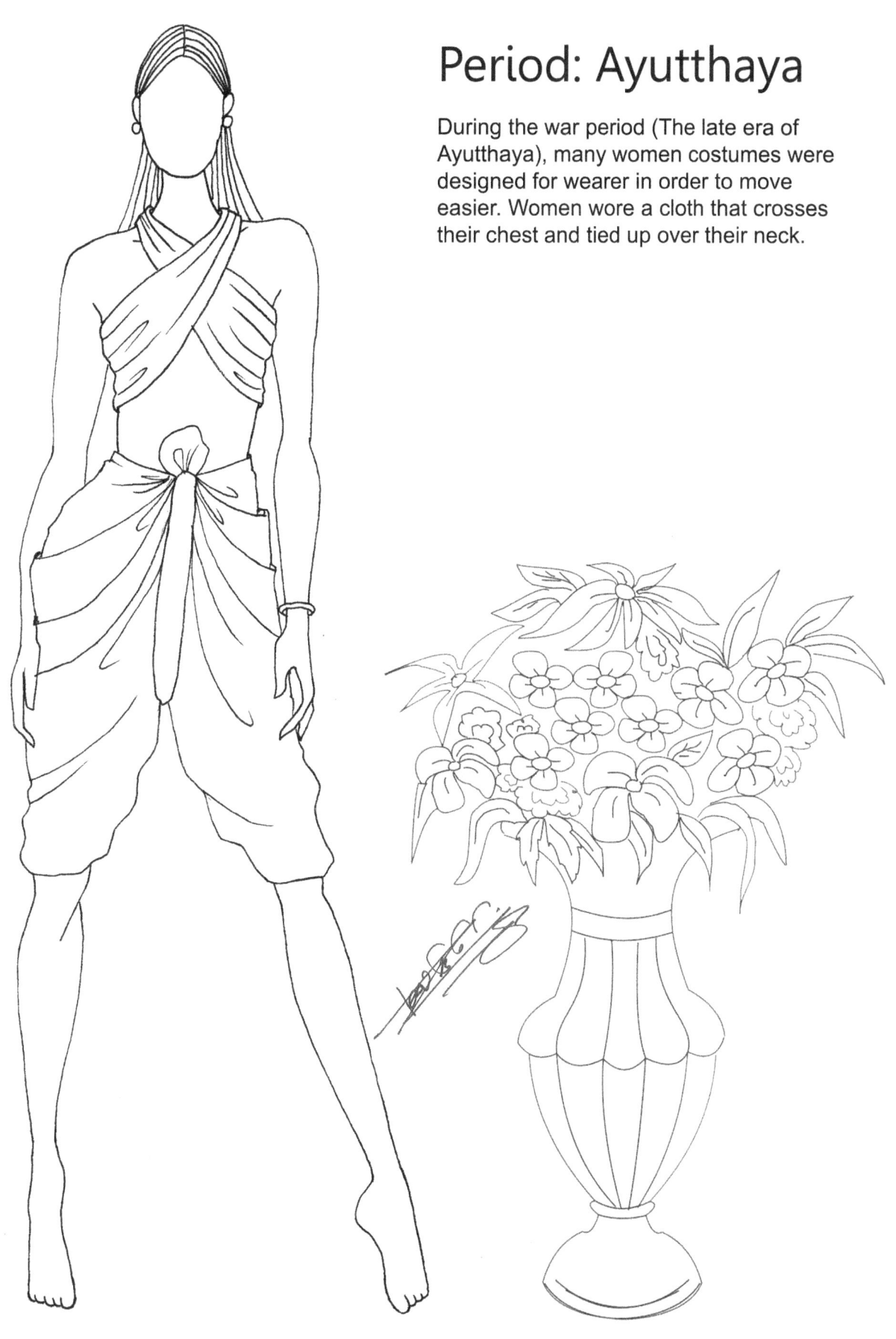

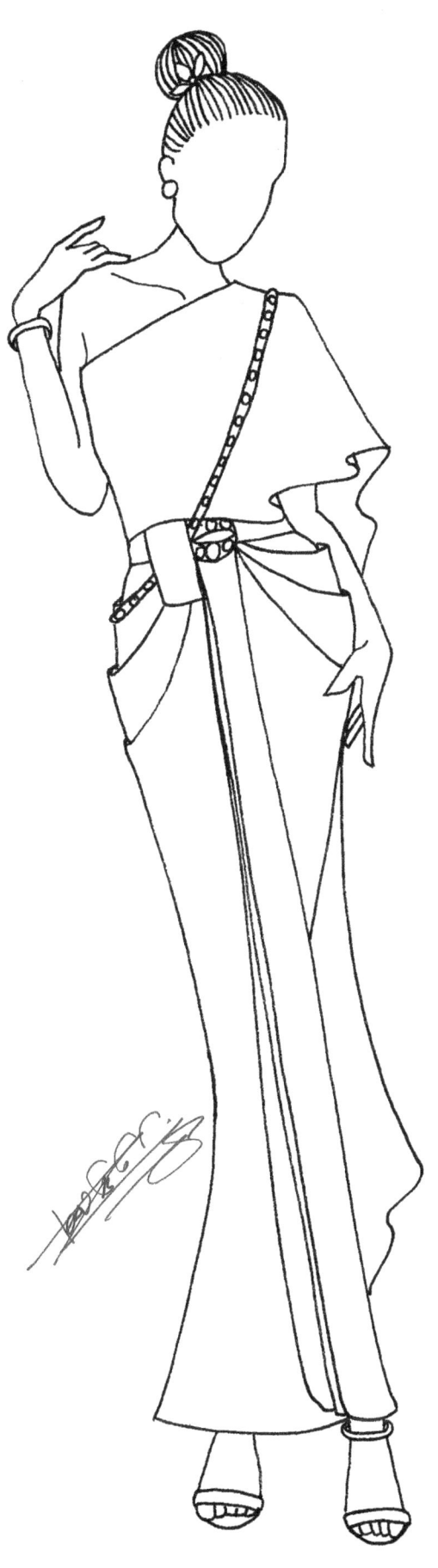

Period: Rama 1

This dress was from the early Rattanakosin periods—King Rama 1 to 4 (1782-1851) with colorful *sabai* (a form of backless shirt) and *na-nang* (a typical Thai wrap skirt). The *sabai* is also known as a long piece of silk, about a foot wide, draped diagonally around the chest by covering one shoulder which drops behind the back.

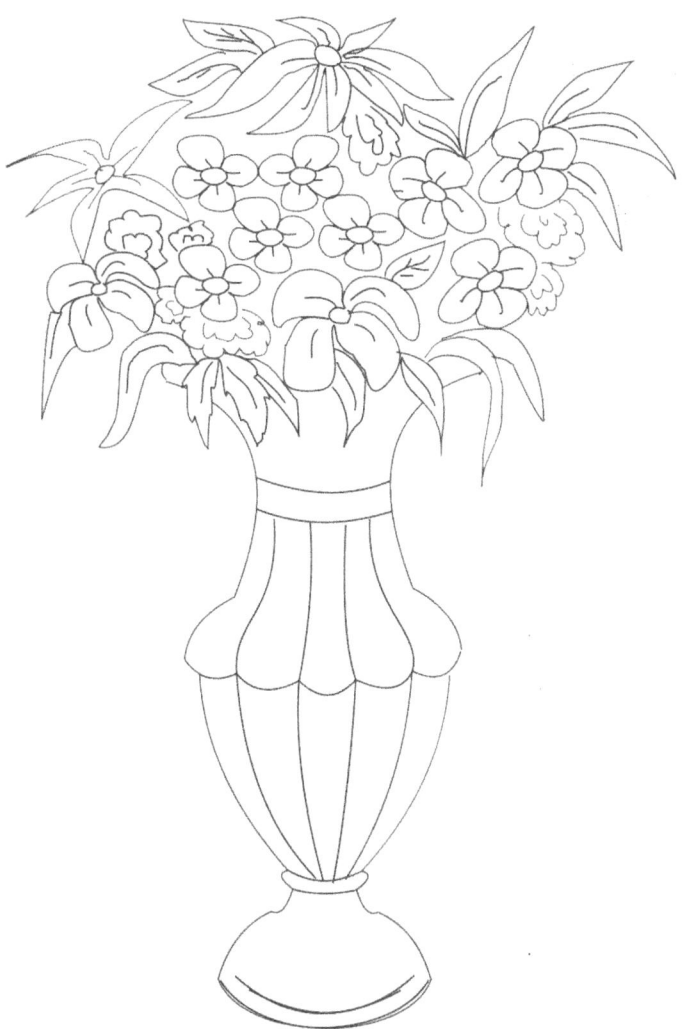

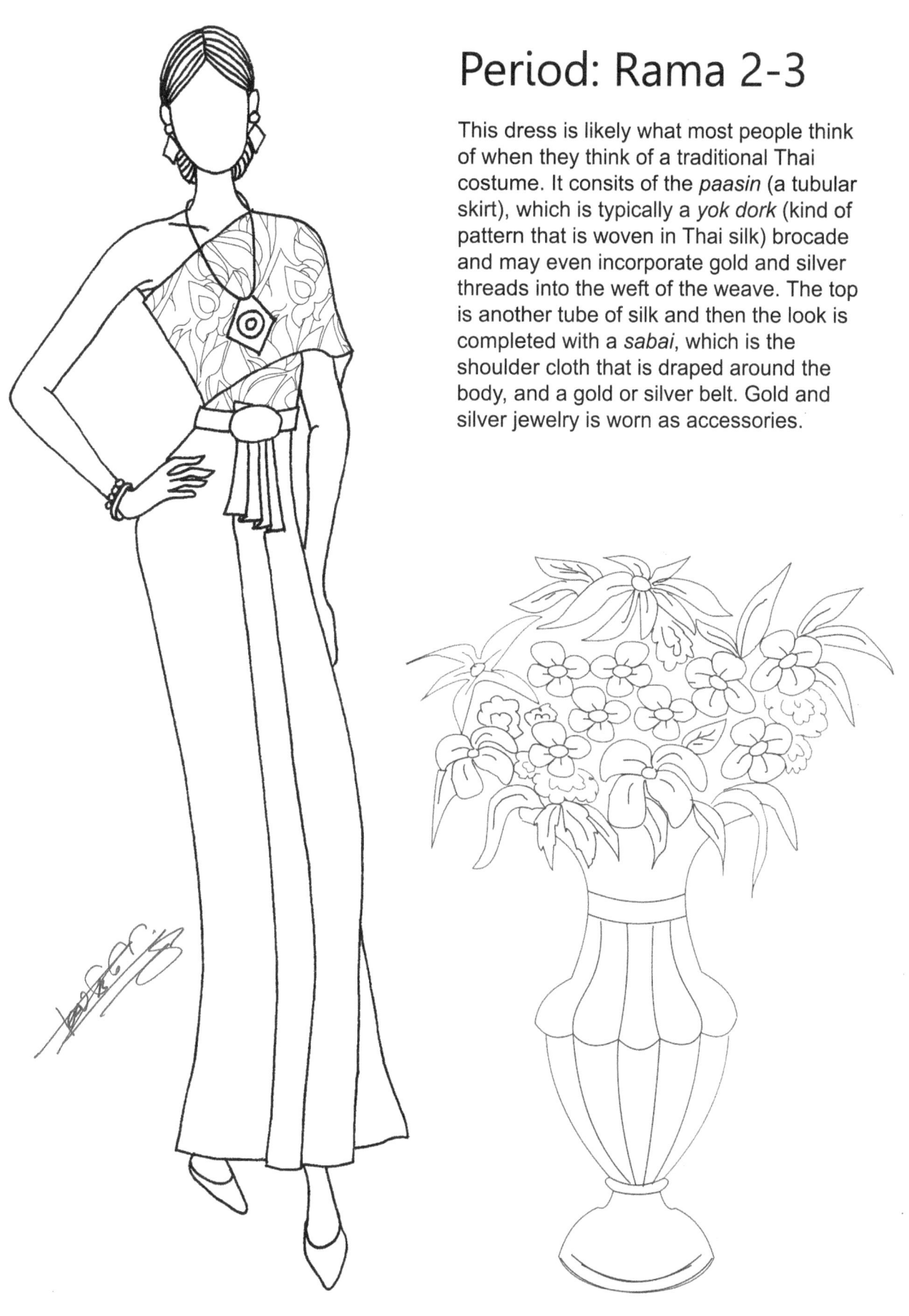

Period: Rama 2-3

This dress is likely what most people think of when they think of a traditional Thai costume. It consits of the *paasin* (a tubular skirt), which is typically a *yok dork* (kind of pattern that is woven in Thai silk) brocade and may even incorporate gold and silver threads into the weft of the weave. The top is another tube of silk and then the look is completed with a *sabai*, which is the shoulder cloth that is draped around the body, and a gold or silver belt. Gold and silver jewelry is worn as accessories.

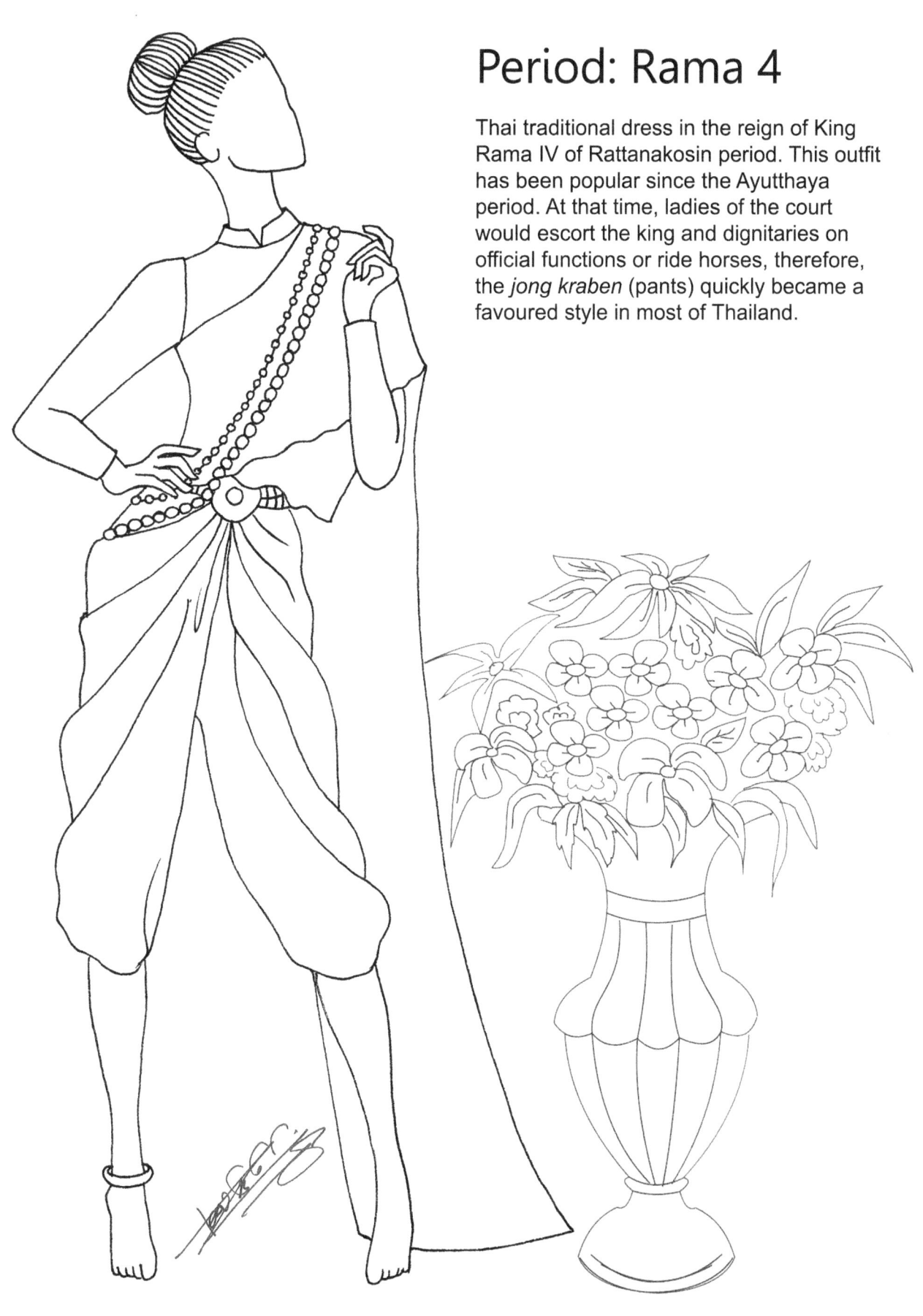

Period: Rama 4

Thai traditional dress in the reign of King Rama IV of Rattanakosin period. This outfit has been popular since the Ayutthaya period. At that time, ladies of the court would escort the king and dignitaries on official functions or ride horses, therefore, the *jong kraben* (pants) quickly became a favoured style in most of Thailand.

Period: Rama 5

From the 1860s, costume in the reign of King Chulalongkorn (Rama V) of Thailand was influenced by the Victorian blouse. Western influence was more apparent during this era. It was worn with the *jong kraben* (pants).

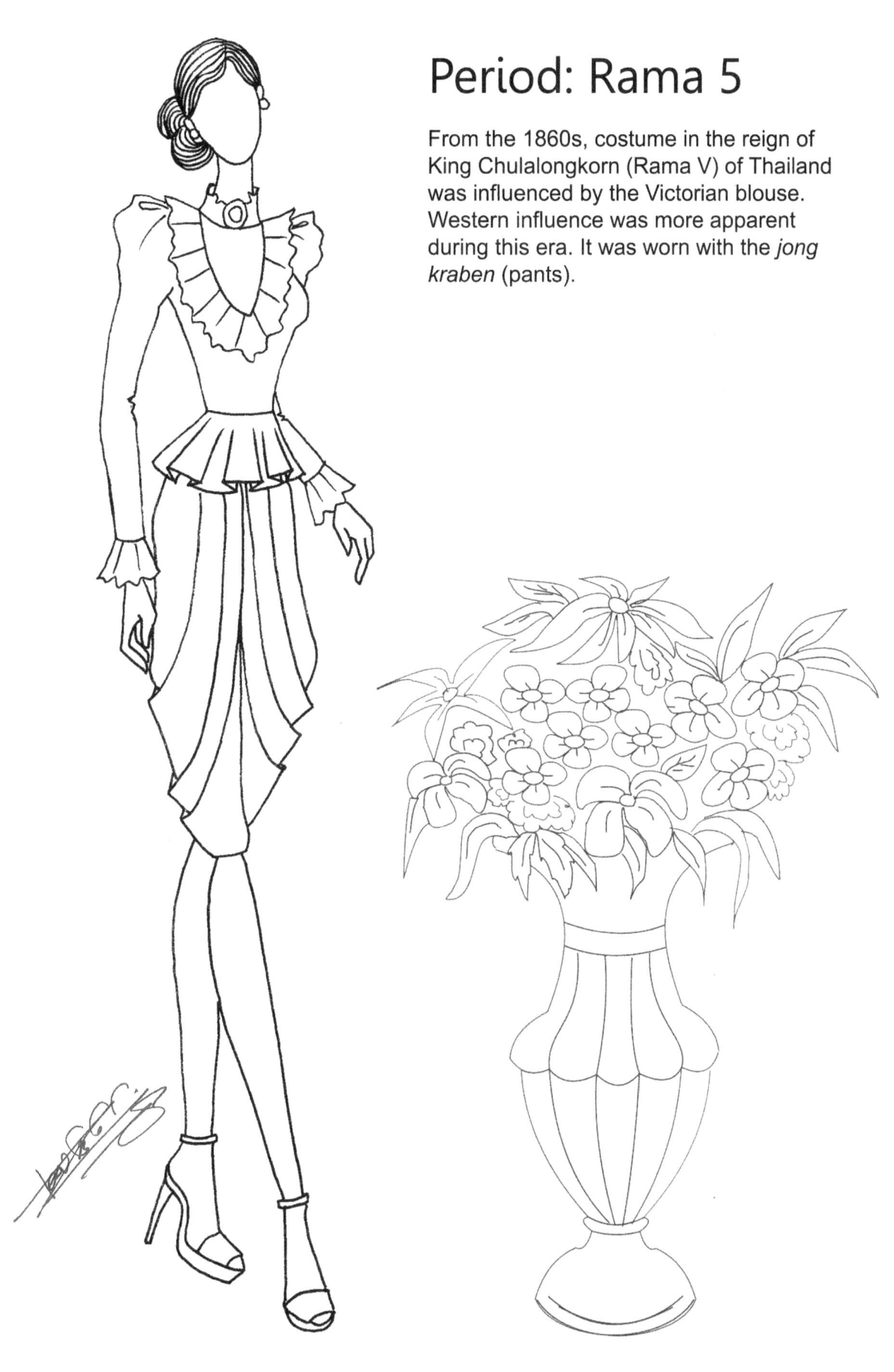

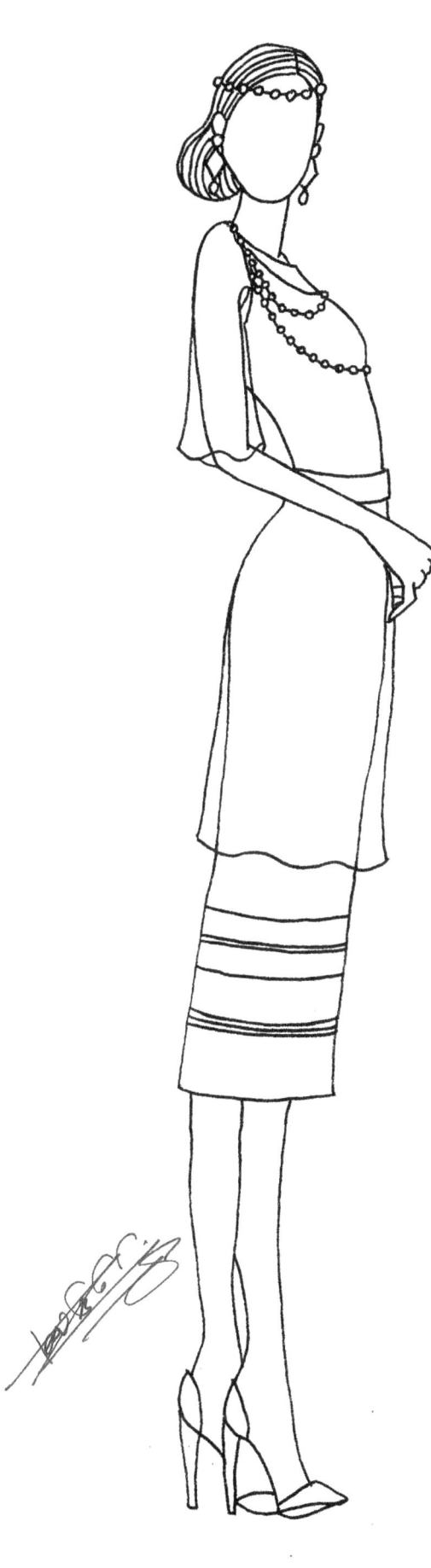

Period: Rama 6

A touch of Western Roaring 20s "Gatsby" is evident in this costume. A laced or see-through long top was worn over a Thai silk dress. A pearl necklace was commonly worn for accessory.

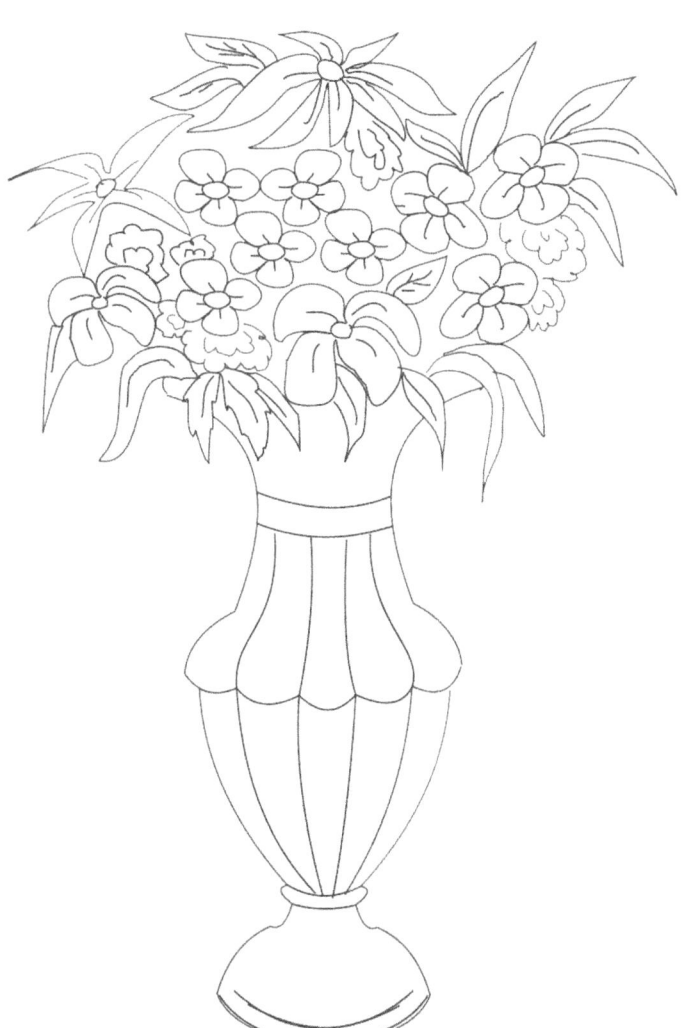

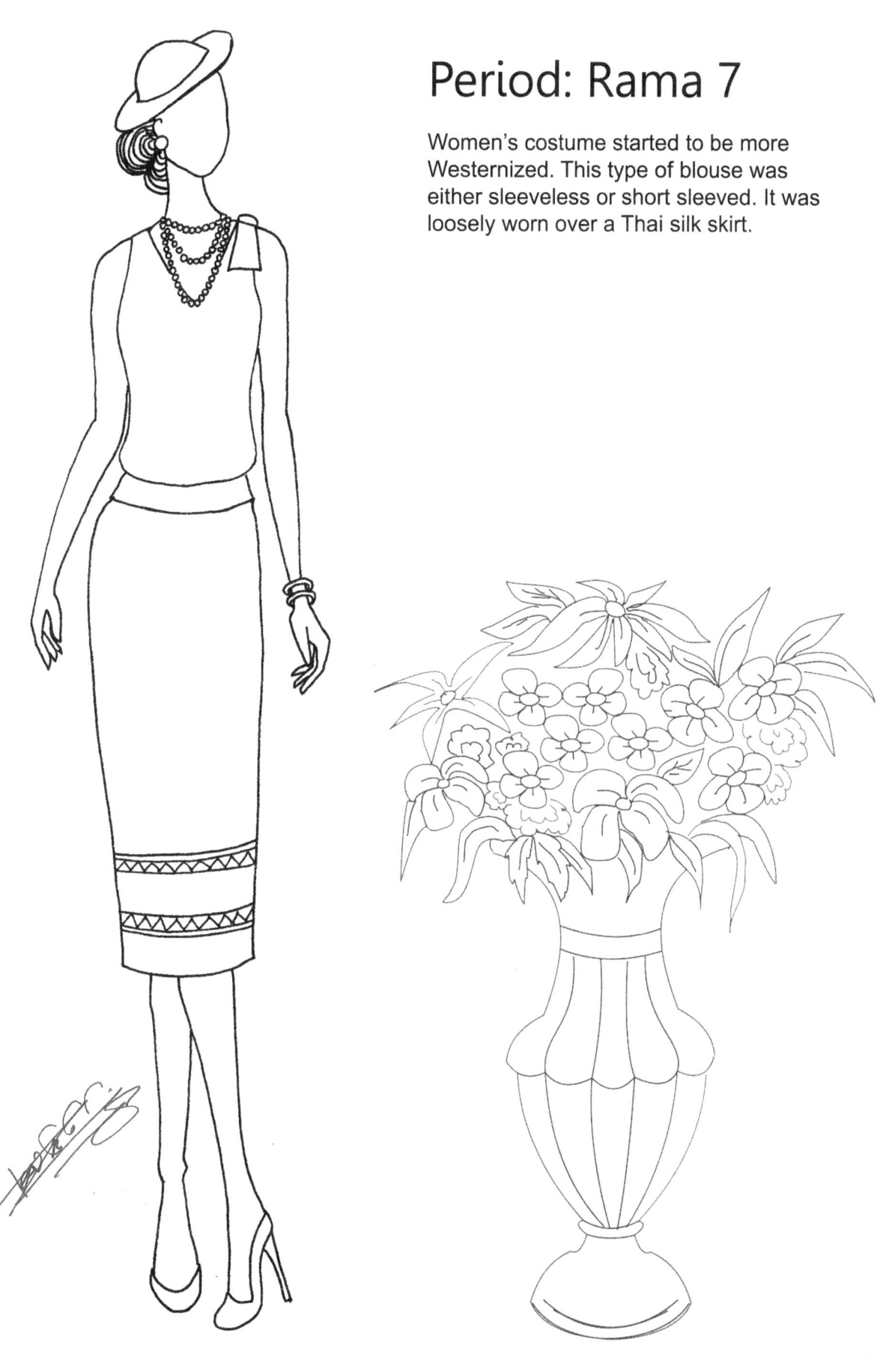

Period: Rama 7

Women's costume started to be more Westernized. This type of blouse was either sleeveless or short sleeved. It was loosely worn over a Thai silk skirt.

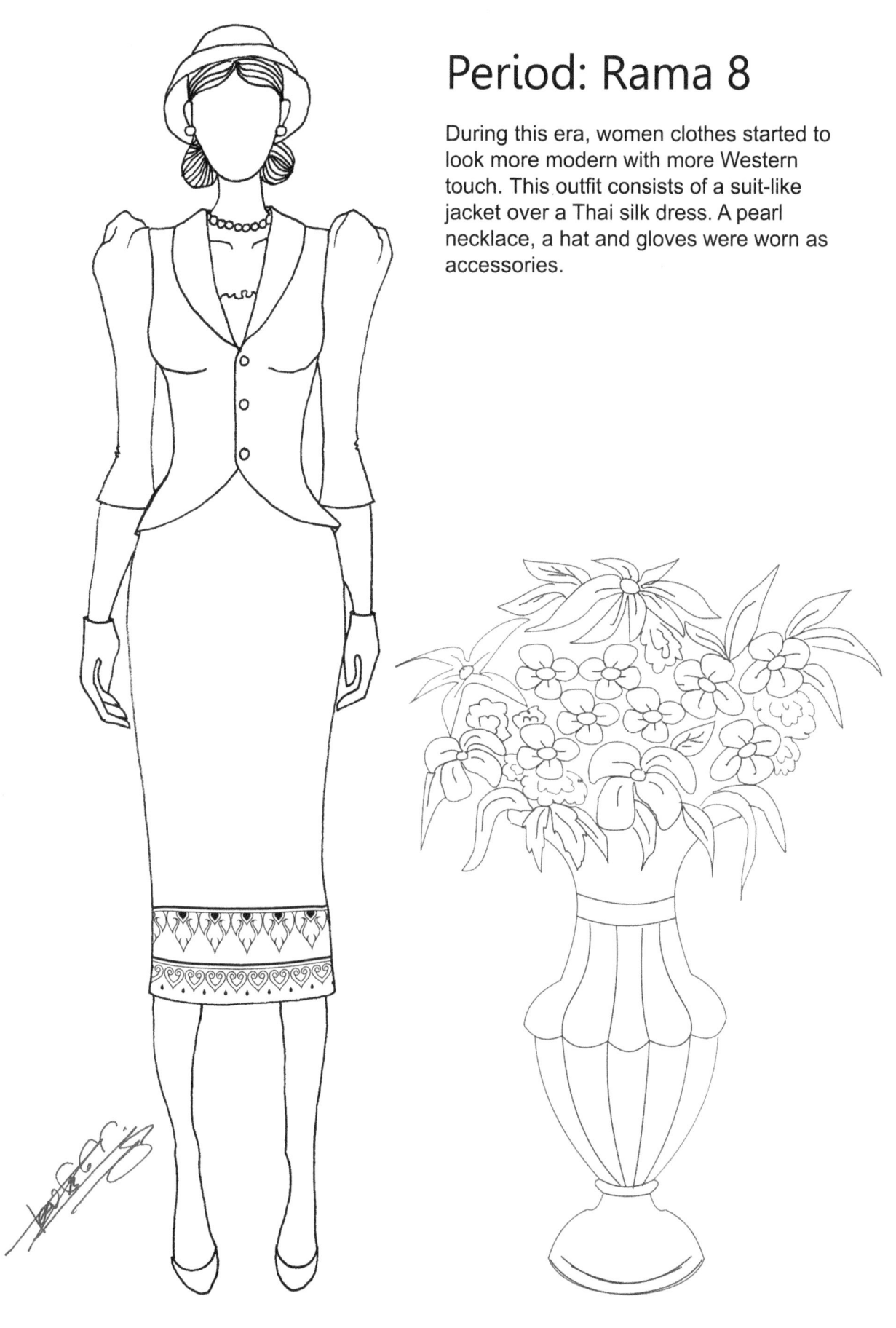

Period: Rama 8

During this era, women clothes started to look more modern with more Western touch. This outfit consists of a suit-like jacket over a Thai silk dress. A pearl necklace, a hat and gloves were worn as accessories.

Period: Rama 9

This outfit is called *Thai Borophiman*. It incorporates a long-sleeved blouse as the top and no *sabai*. The buttons for the round-necked blouse can be either in the front or the back and sometimes the pieces are sewn together into a dress. Again, completed with a gold or silver belt and accessorized with gold or silver jewelry.

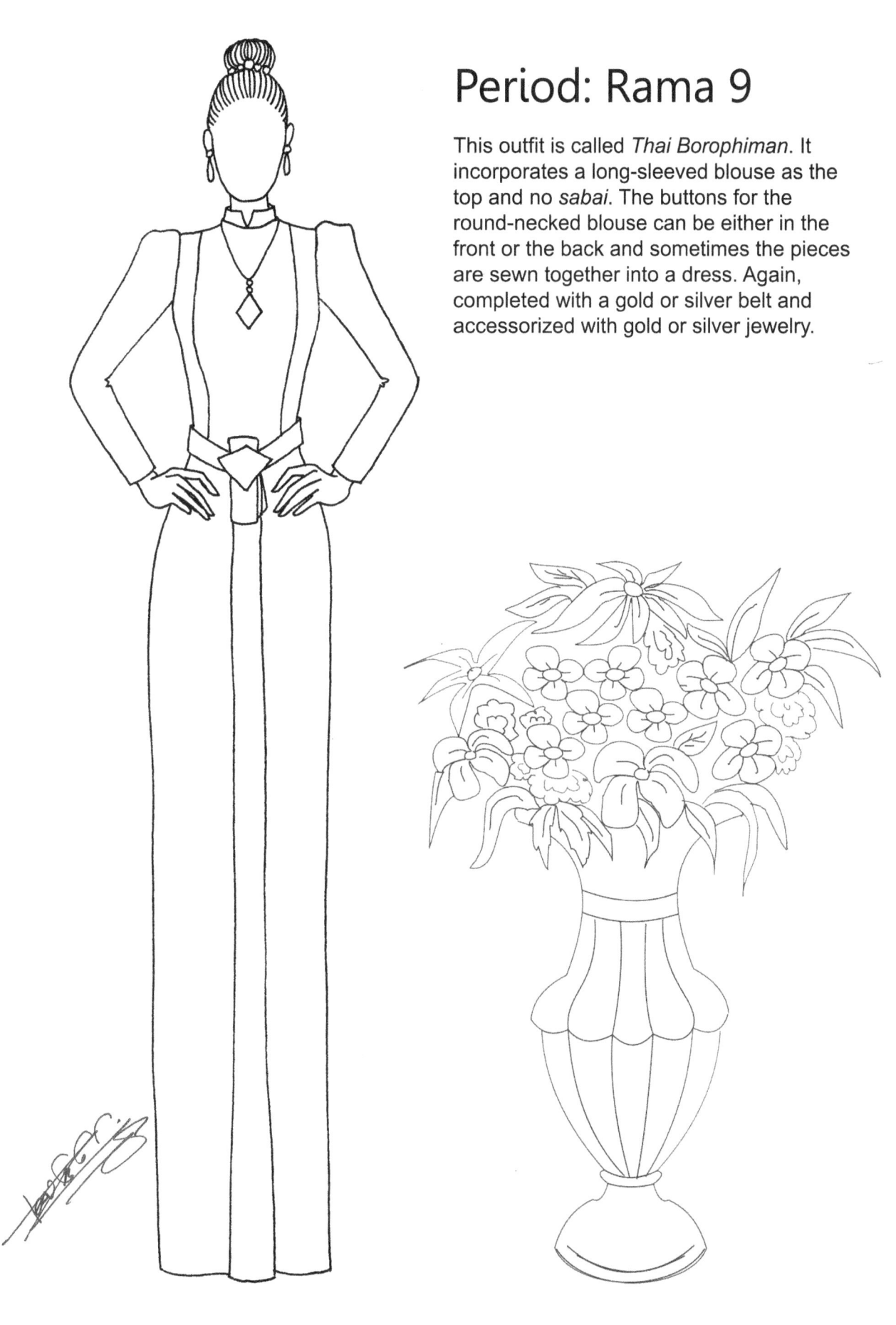

Thai Dusit

This style of outfit is considered the most modern. It is clearly a mix of Thai and Western style and is intended to be worn to events that would usually call for Western-style evening wear. It is a slim-fitting dress made with a brocaded silk and accessorized with either traditional Thai or Western jewelry.

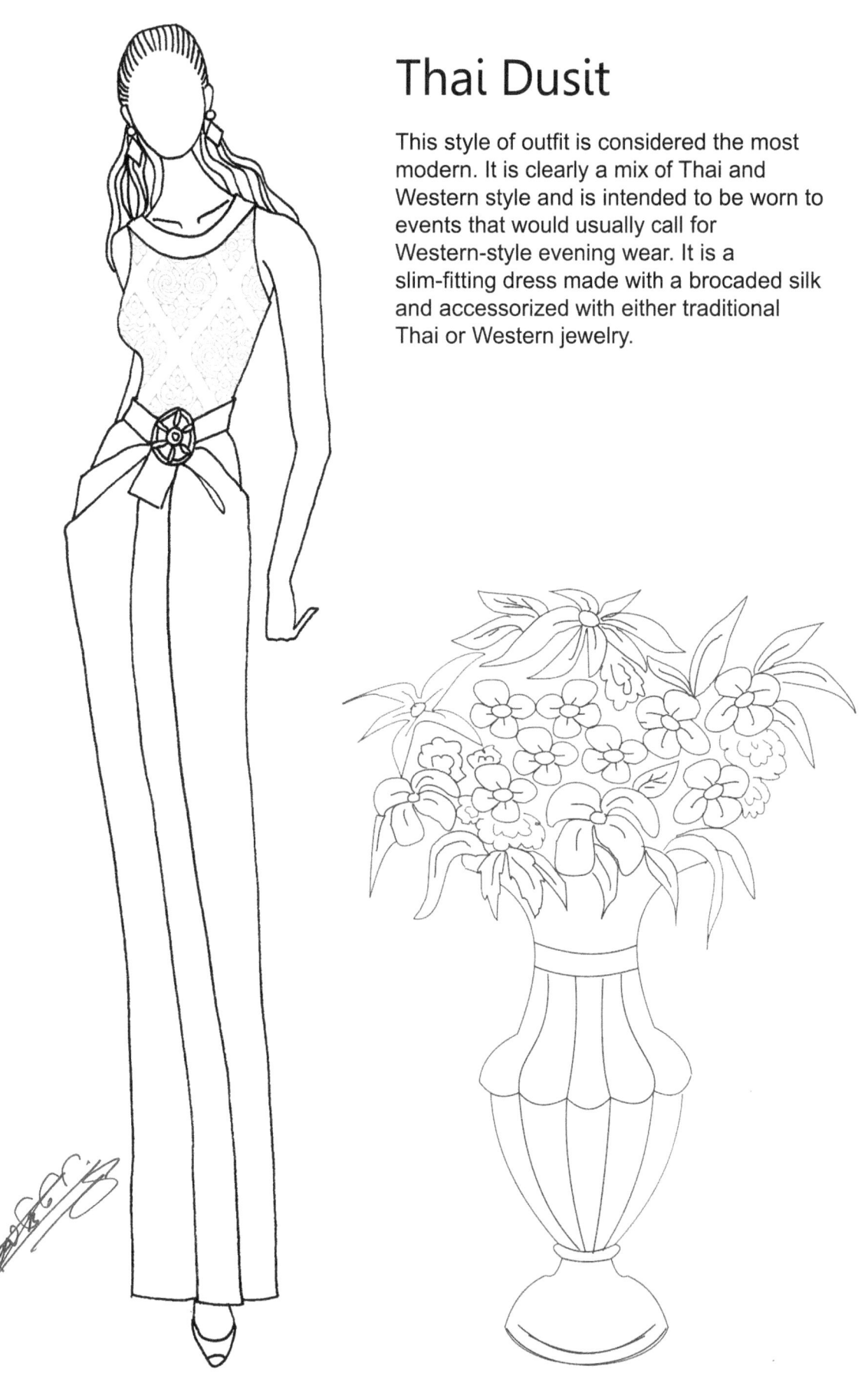

Modern Thai Dress

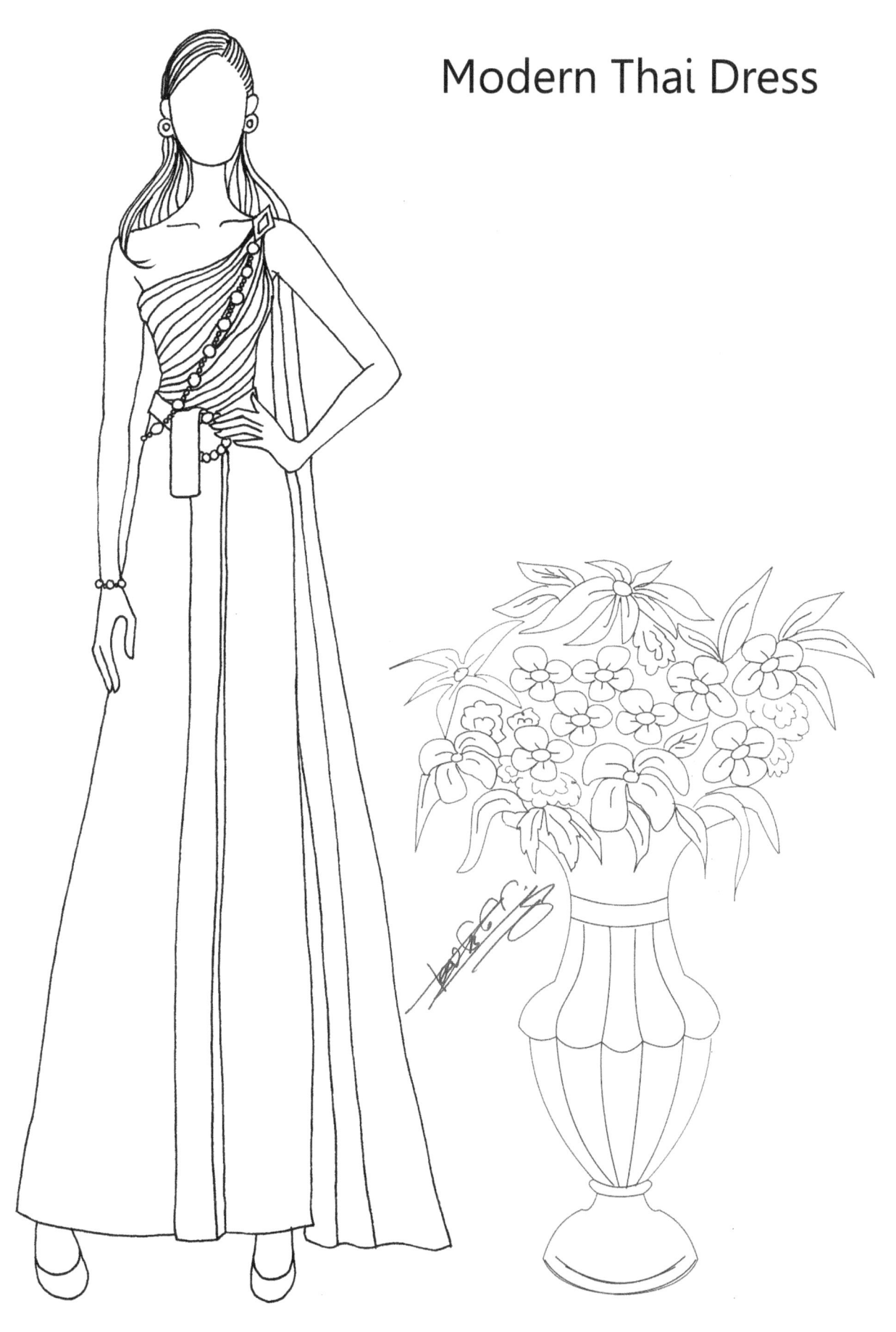

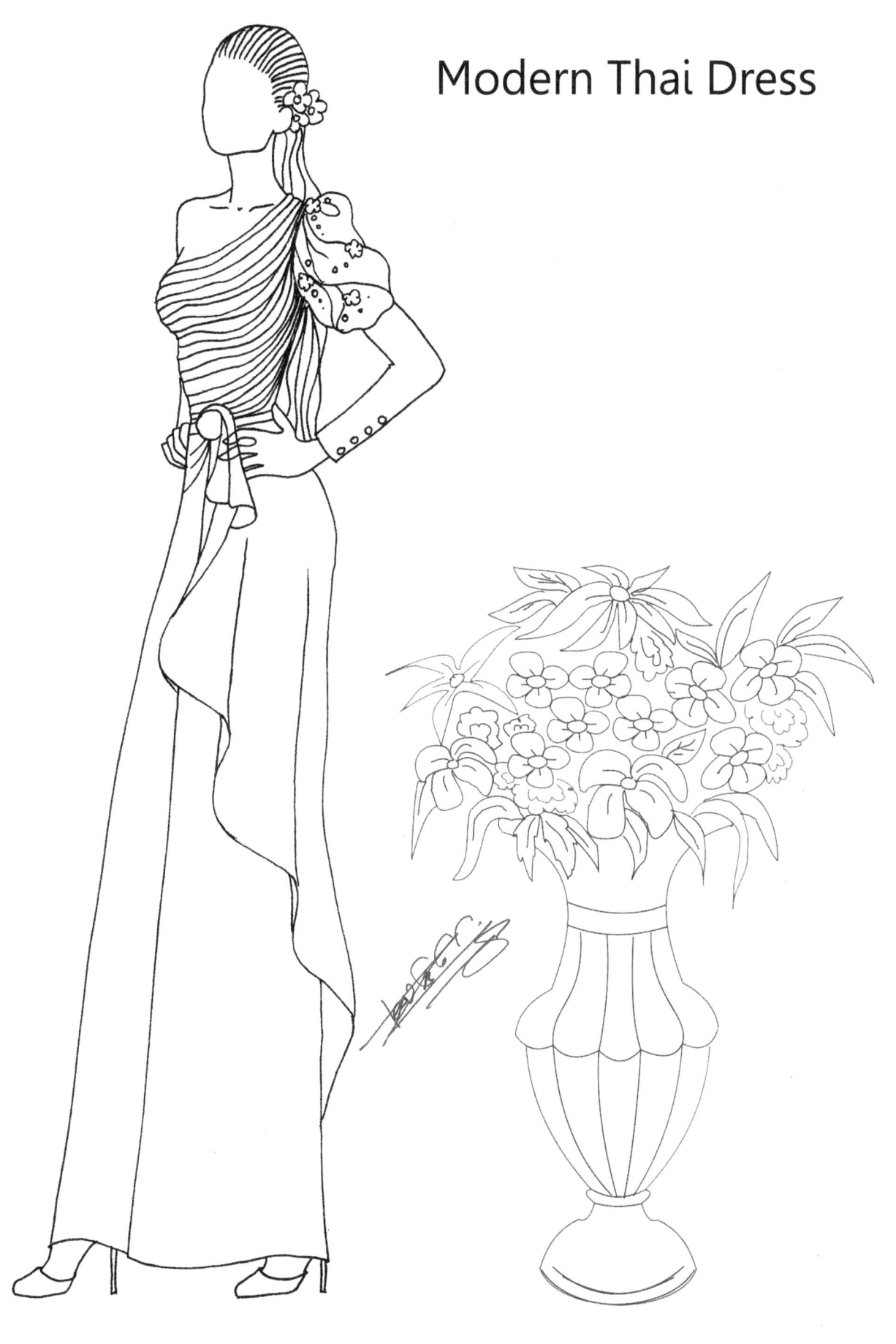

Modern Thai Dress

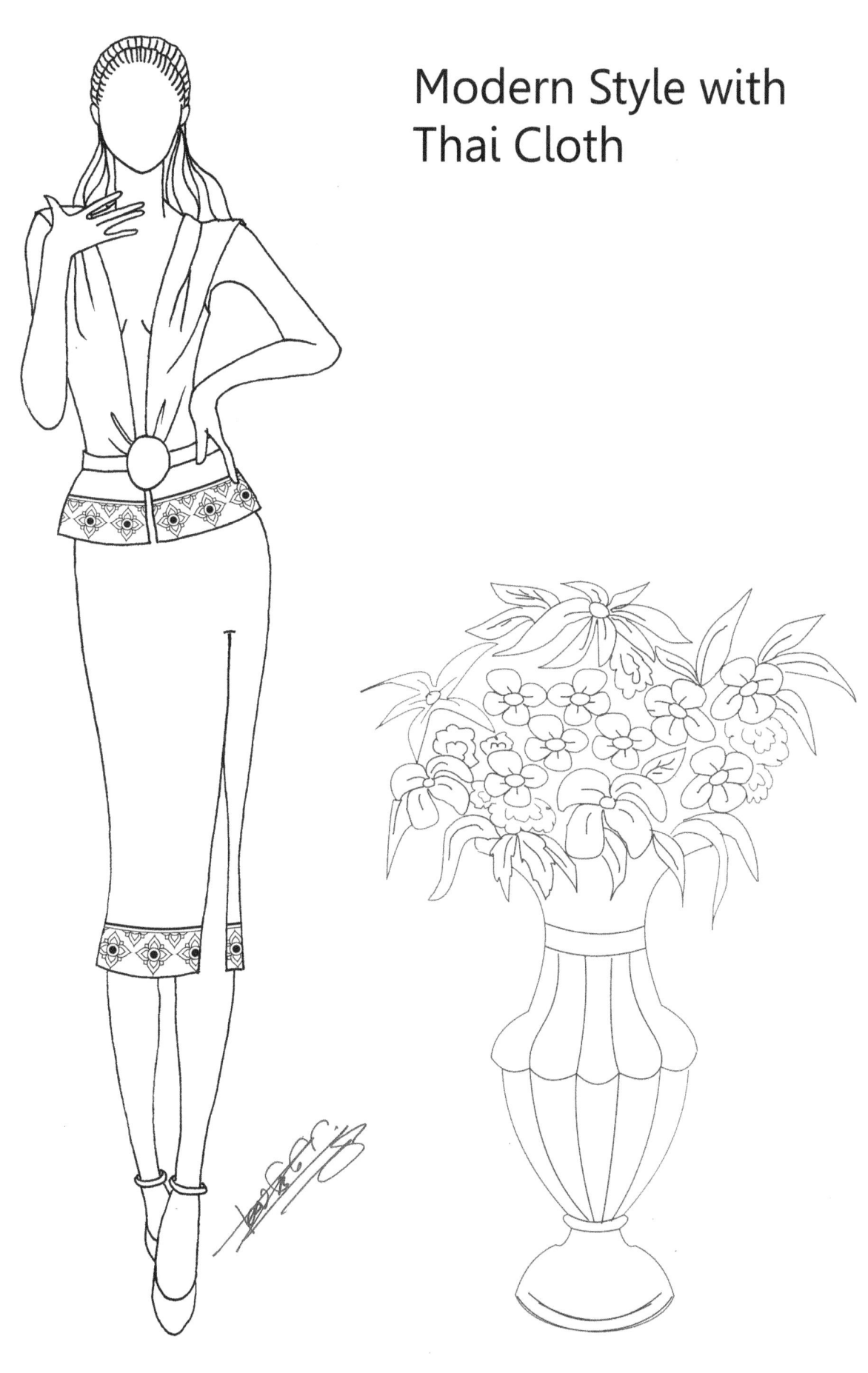

Modern Style with Thai Cloth

Modern Style Top with Thai Style Skirt and Pattern

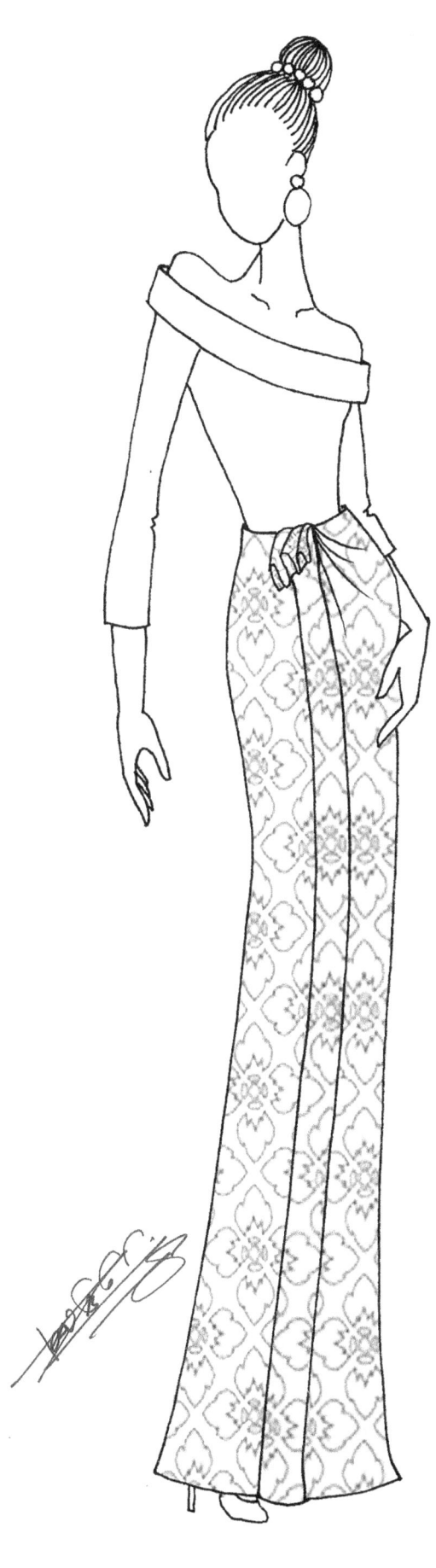
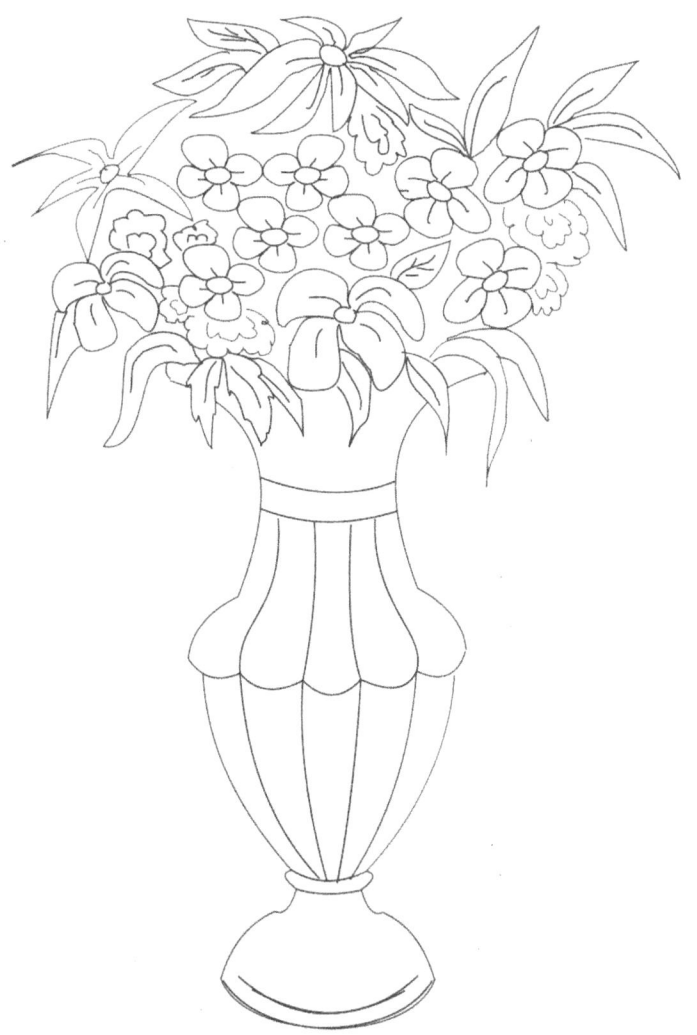

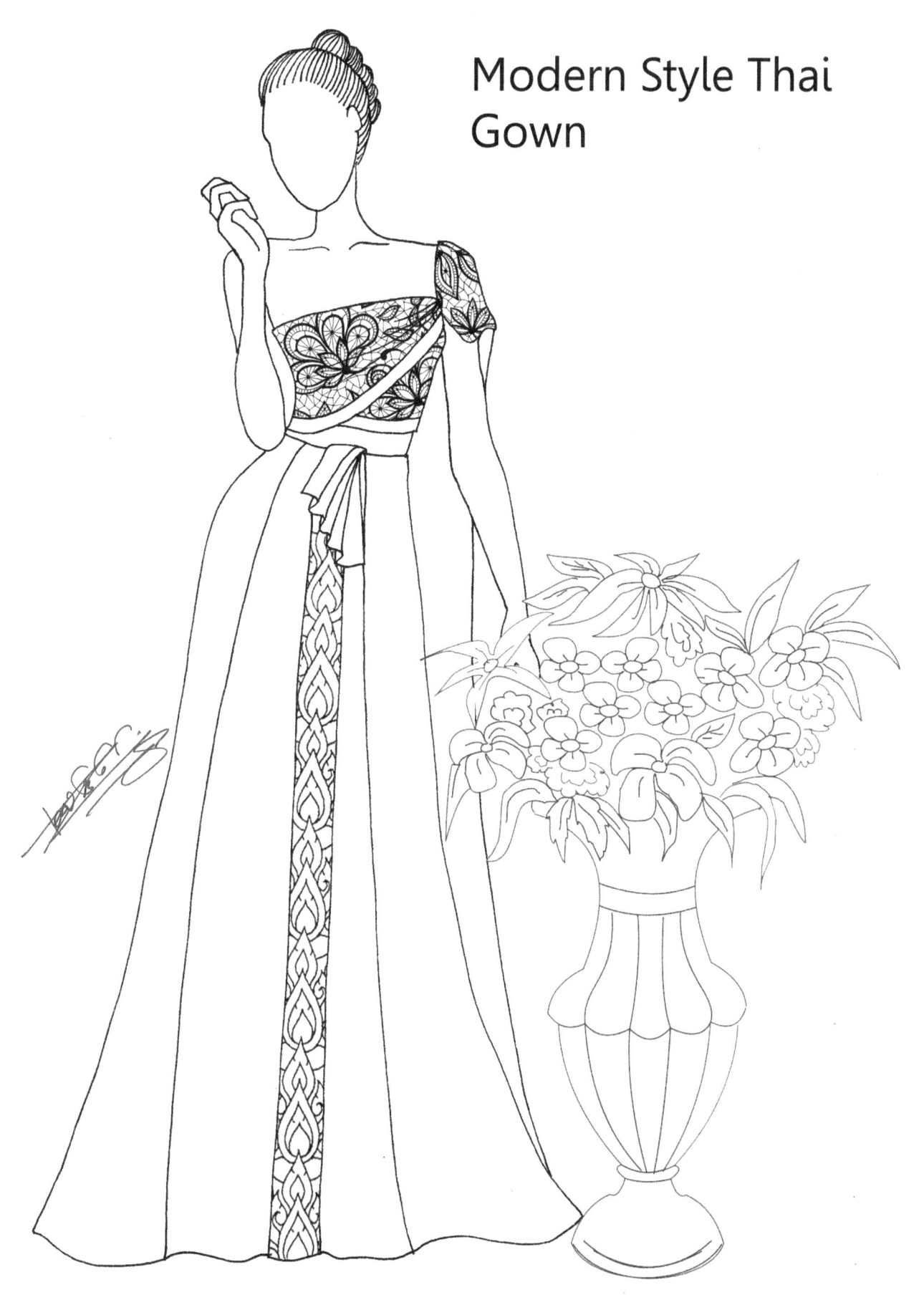

Modern Style Thai Gown

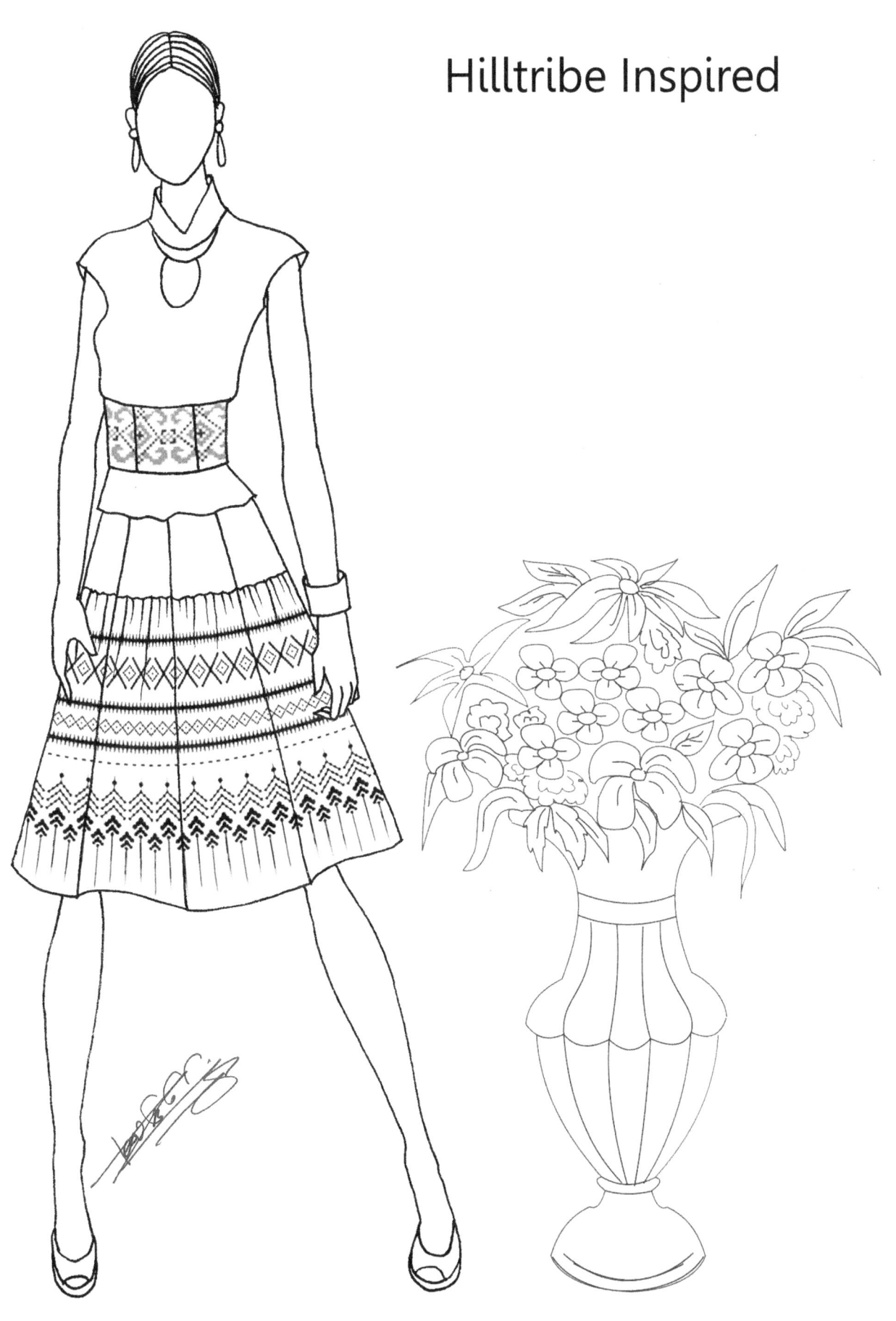

Hilltribe Inspired

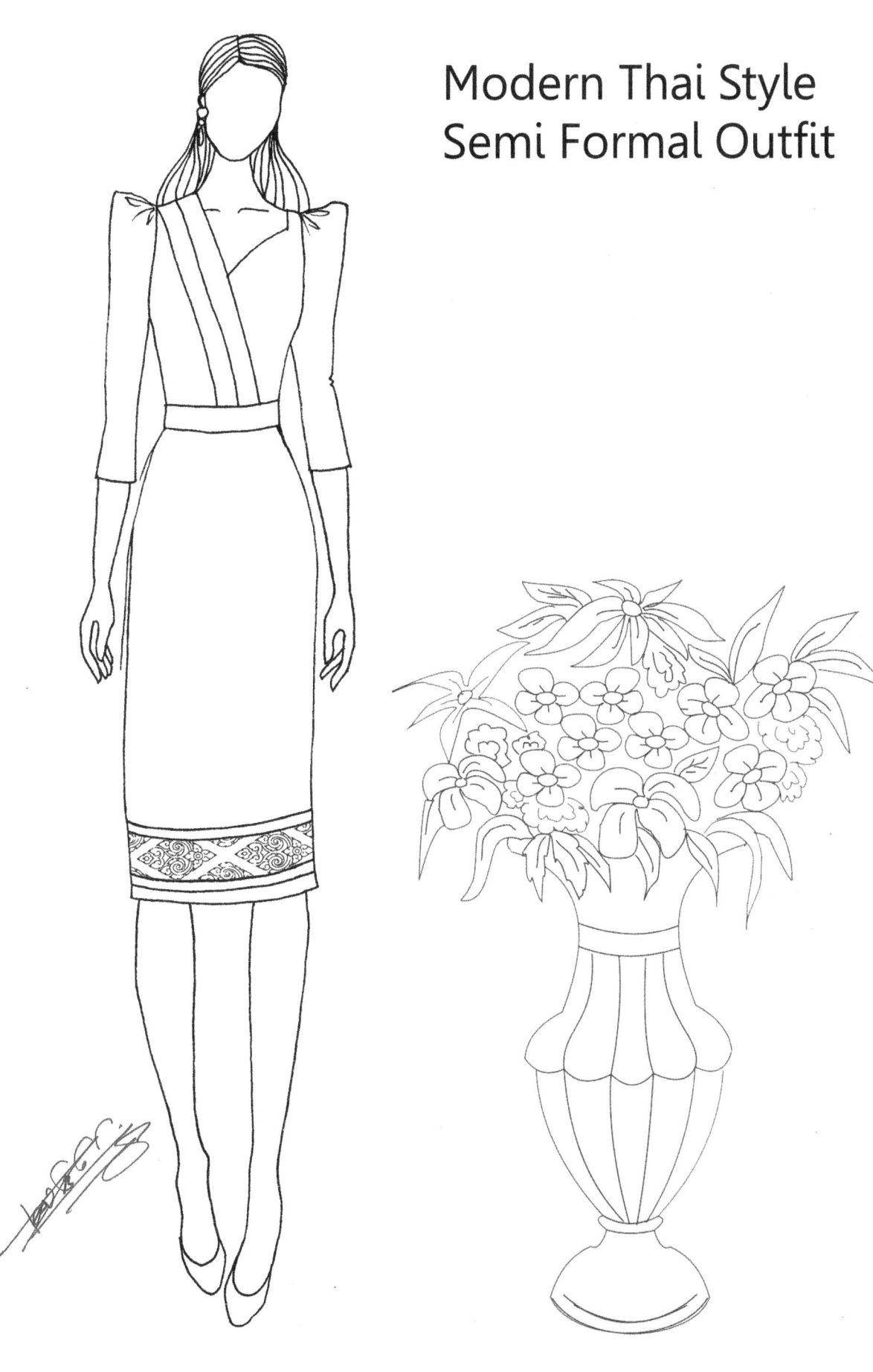

Modern Thai Style Semi Formal Outfit

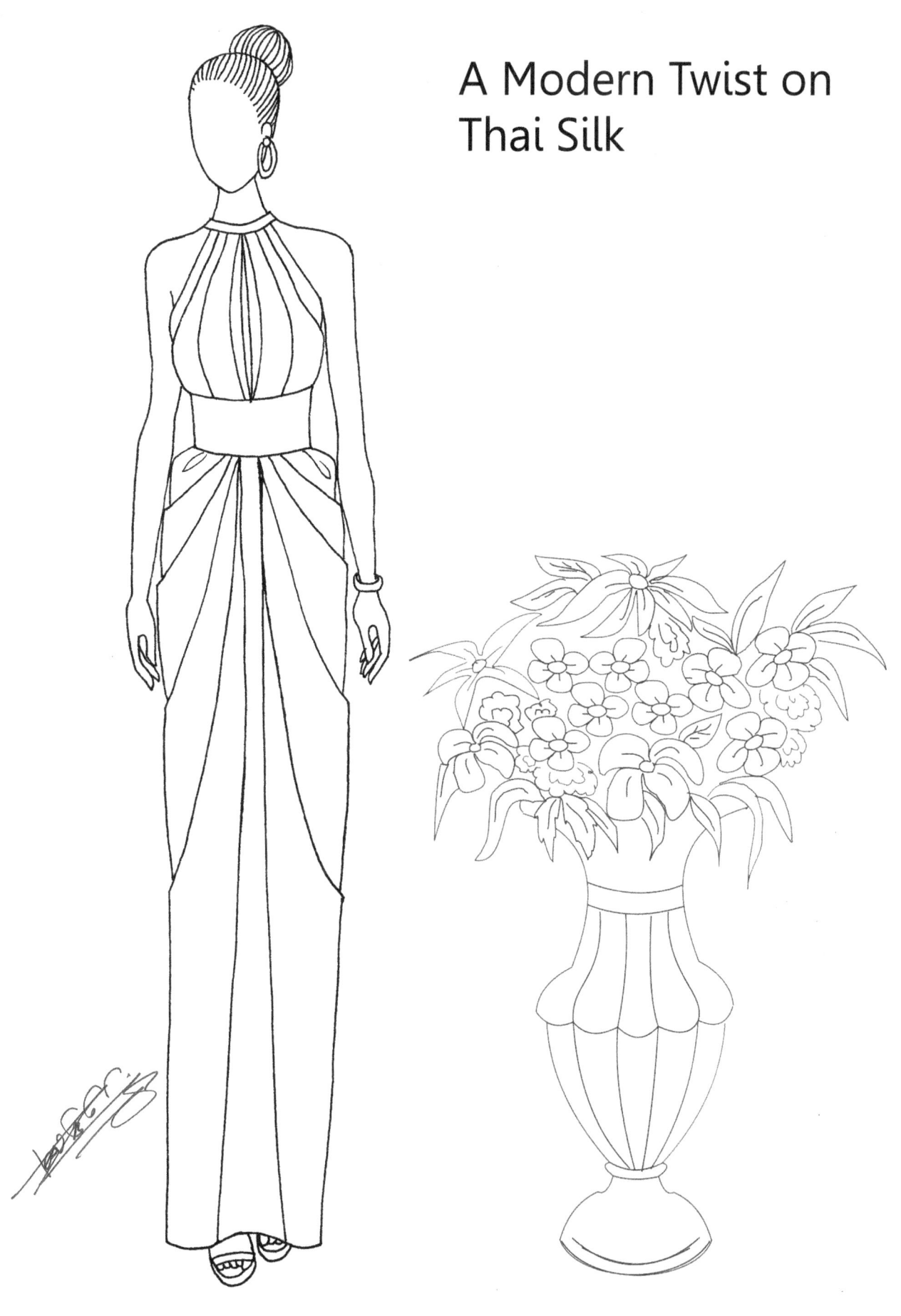

A Modern Twist on Thai Silk

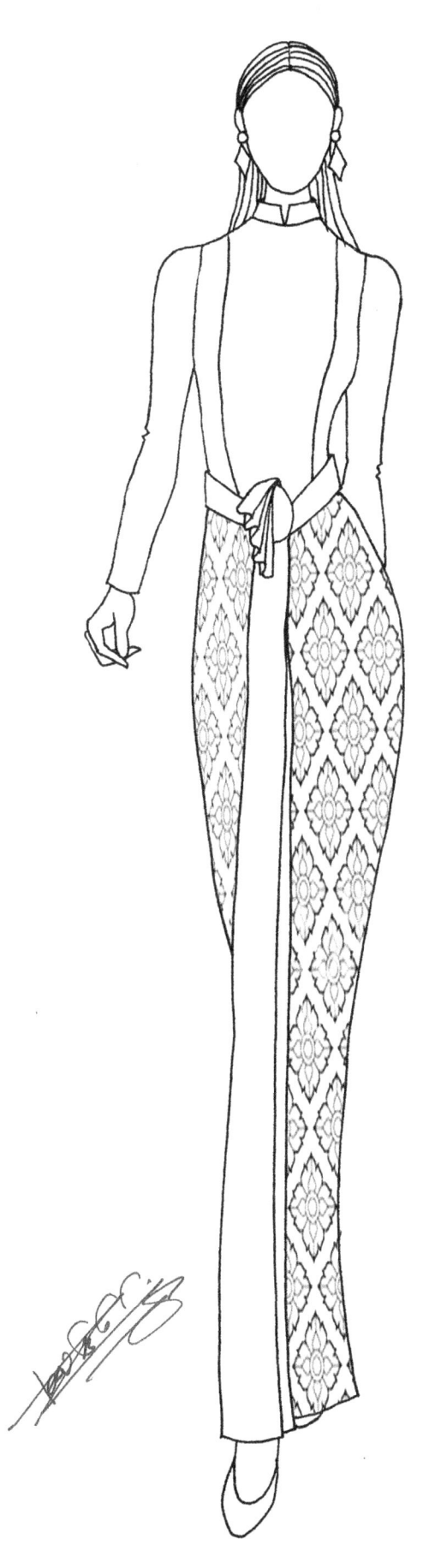

Classic Thai Borophiman

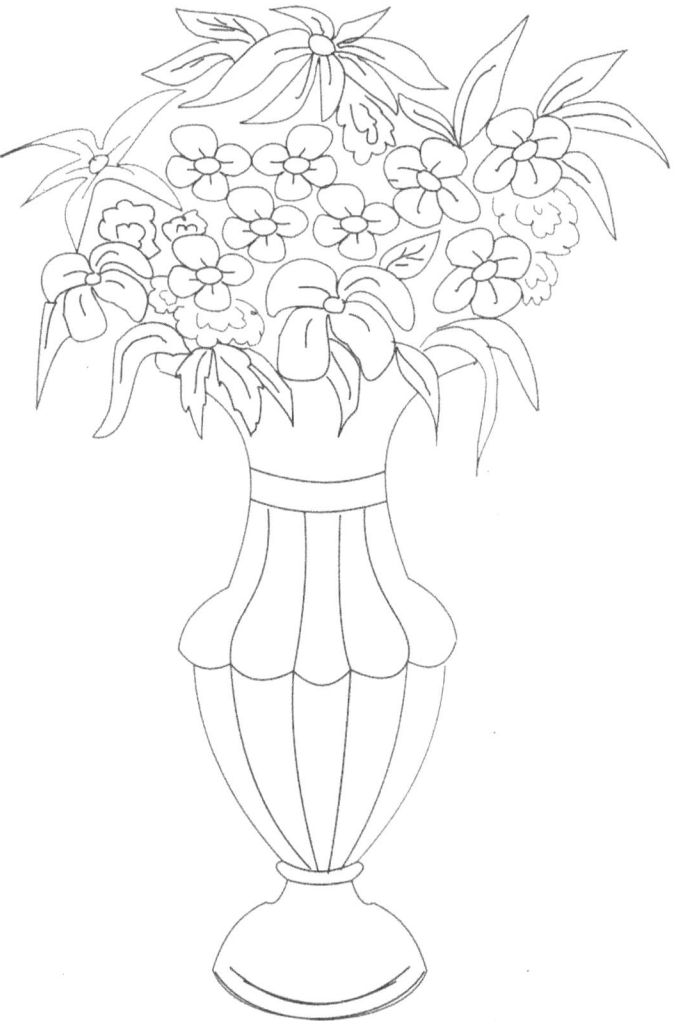

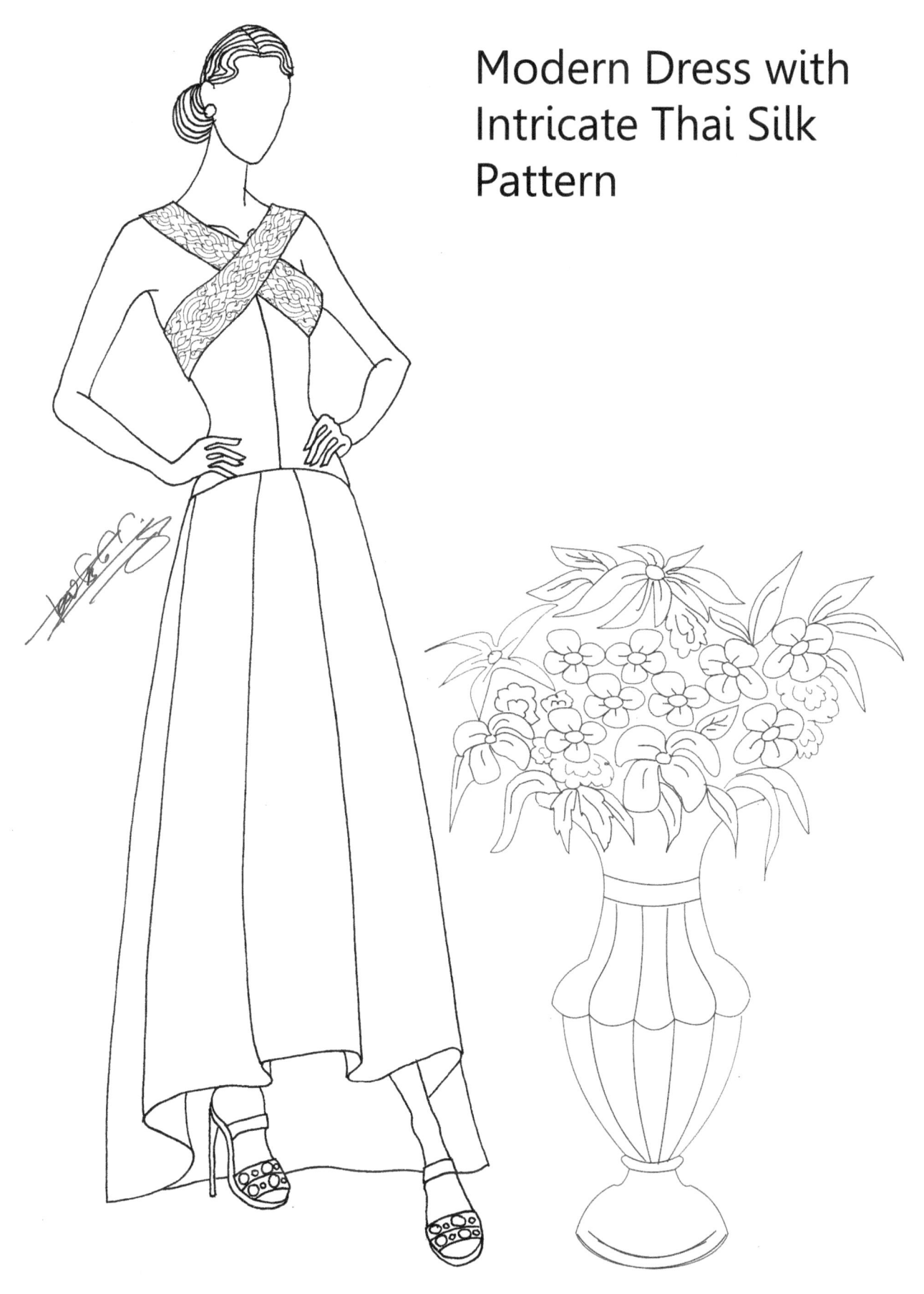

Modern Dress with Intricate Thai Silk Pattern

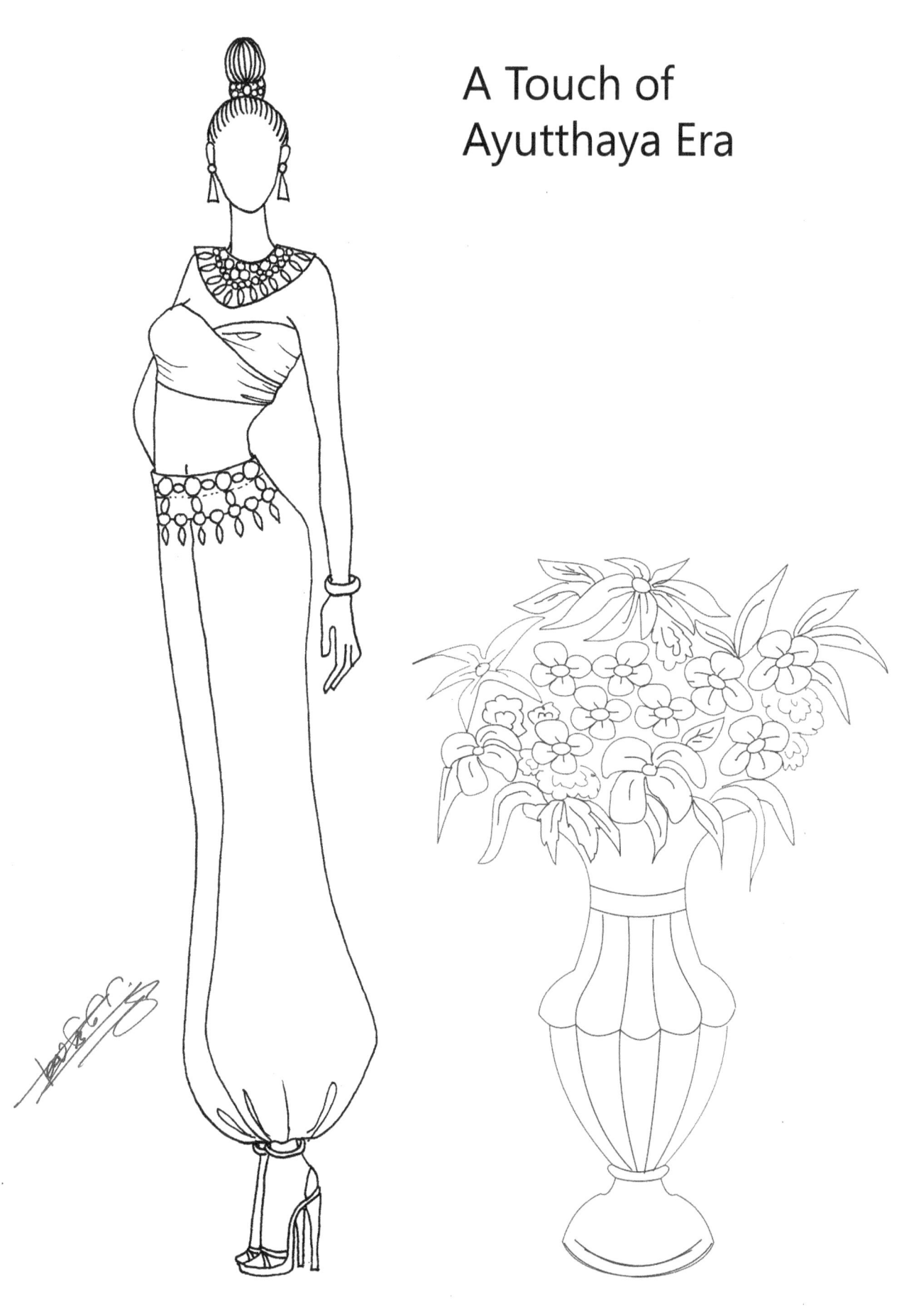

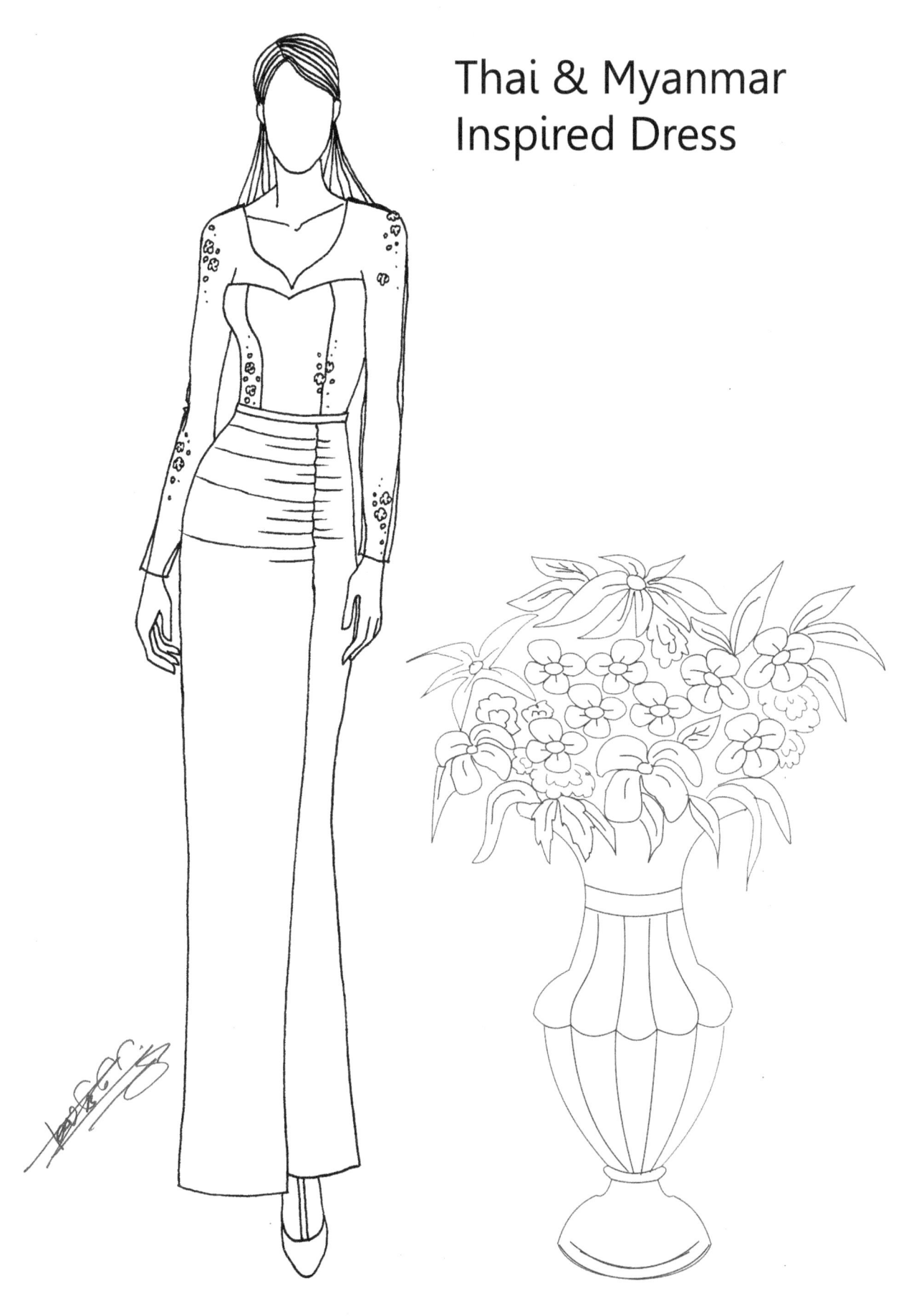

Thai & Myanmar Inspired Dress

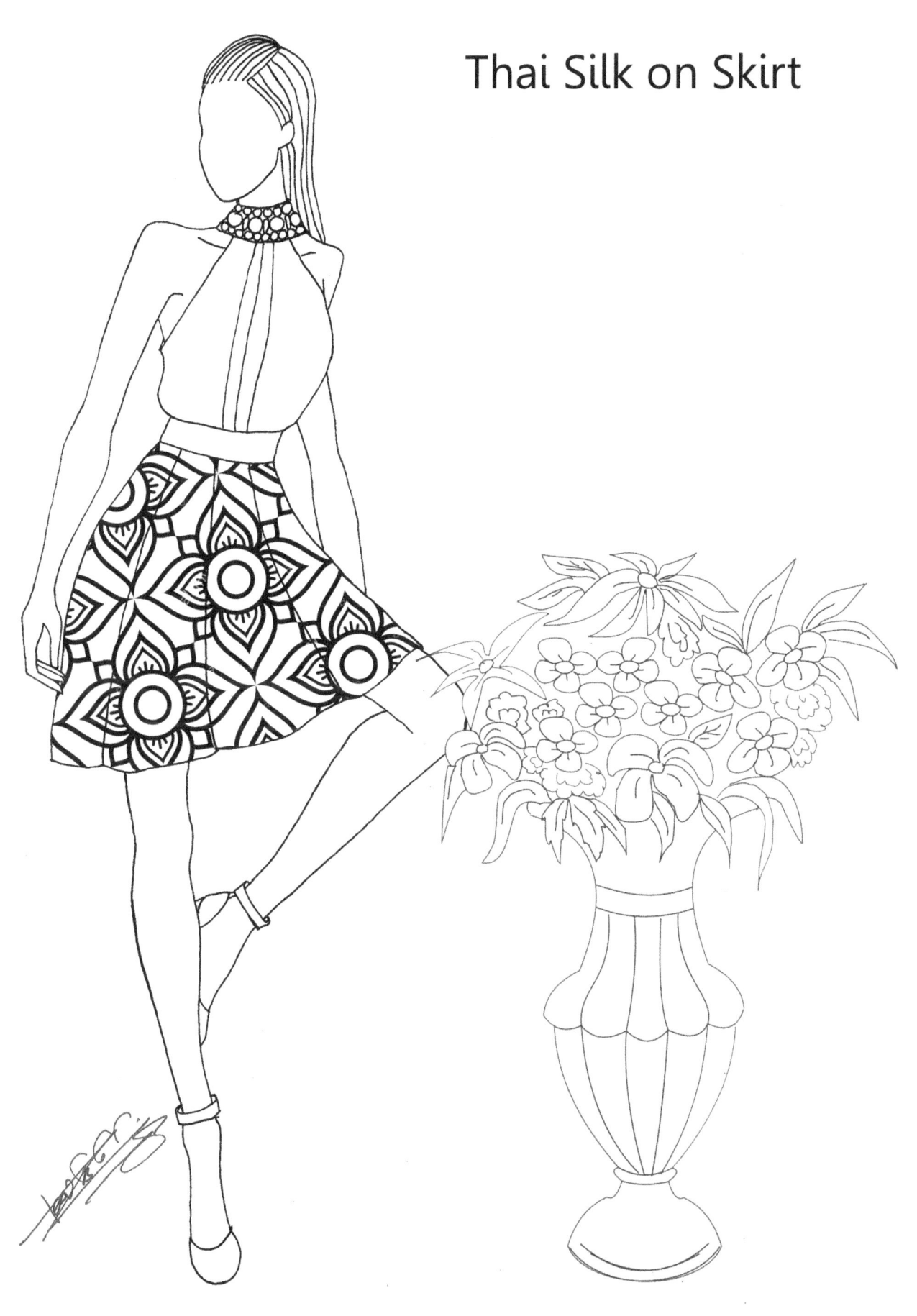

Thai Silk on Skirt

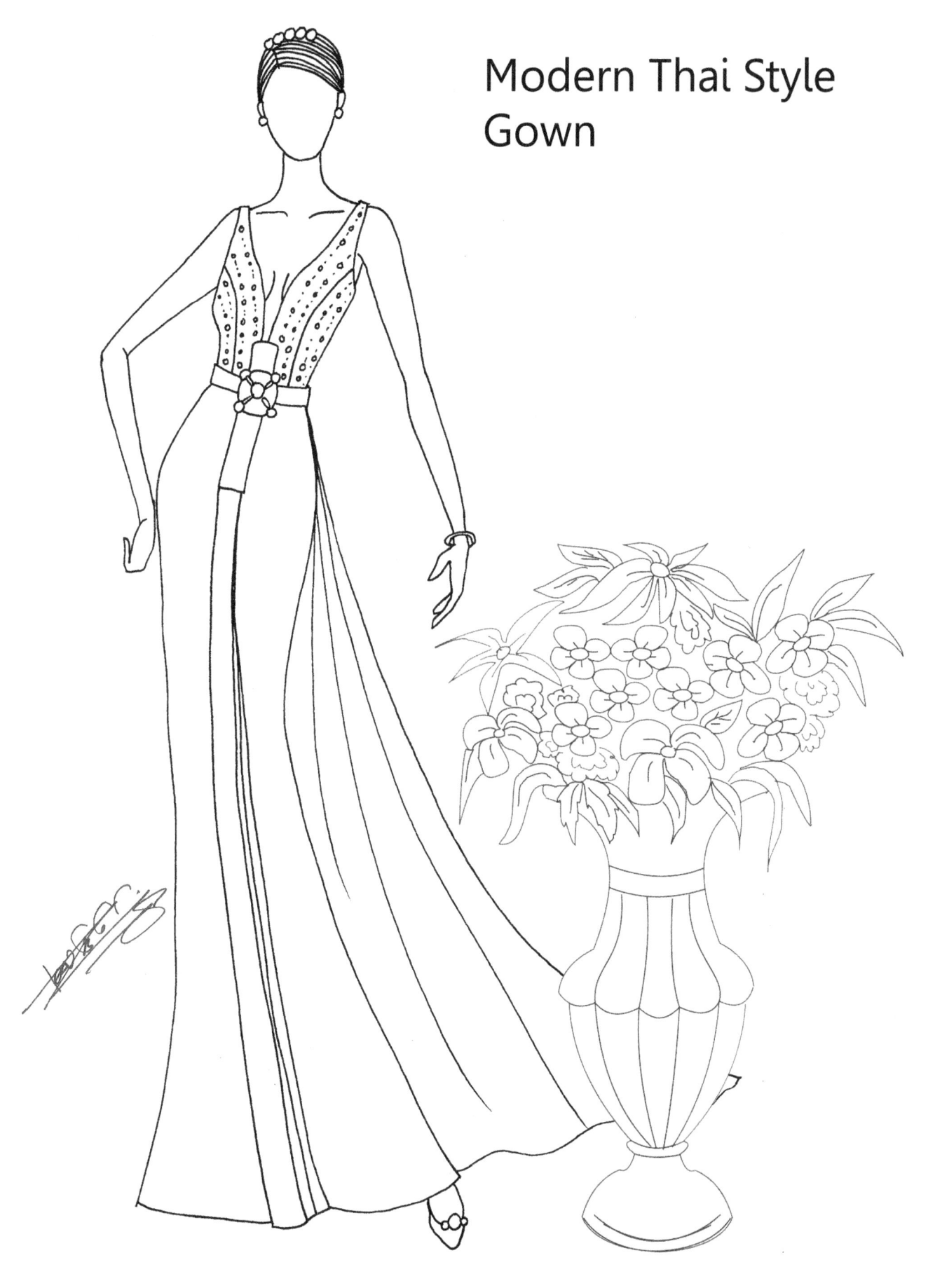

Modern Thai Style Gown

Yok Dork Pattern on Skirt

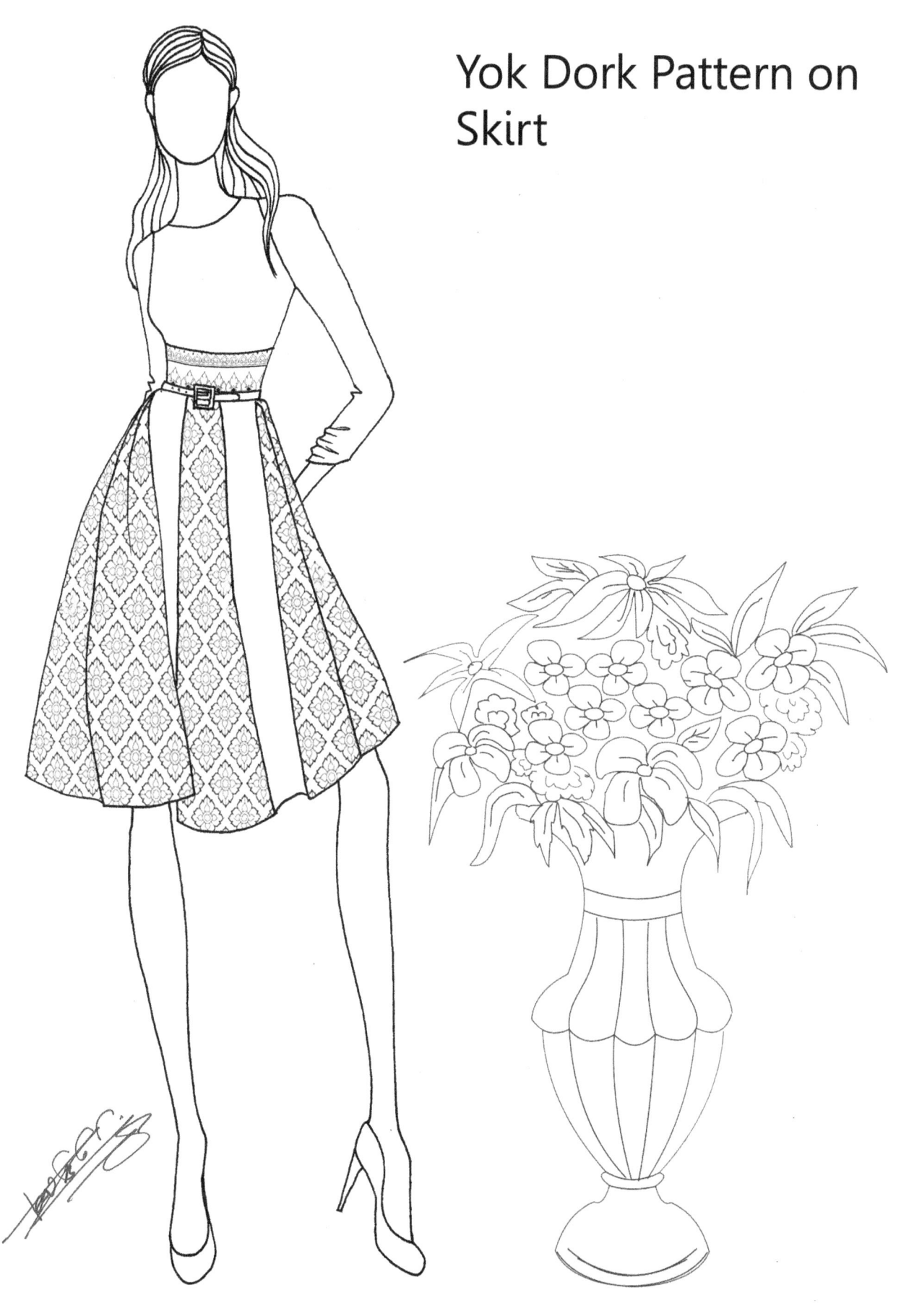

Hilltribe Pattern

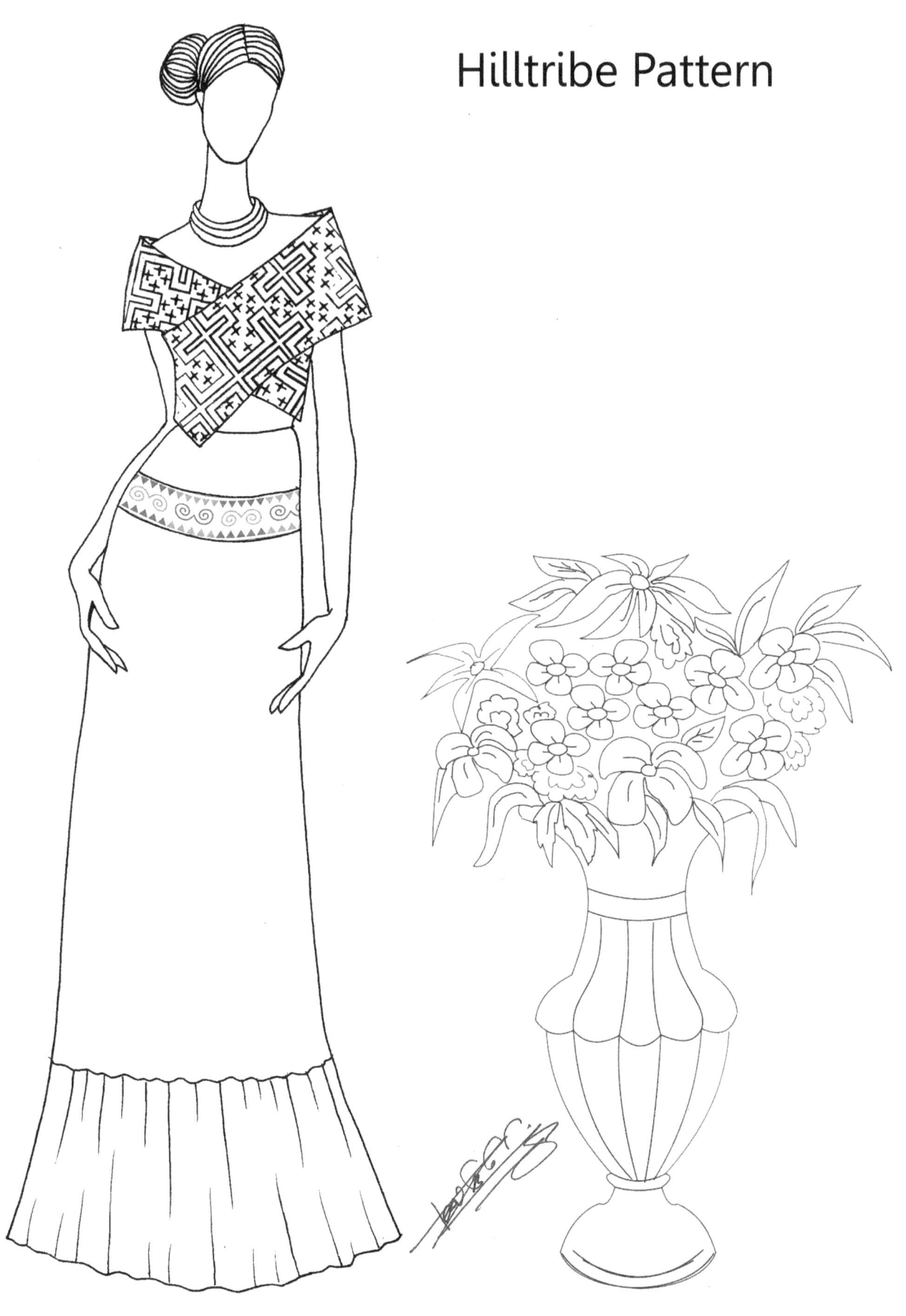

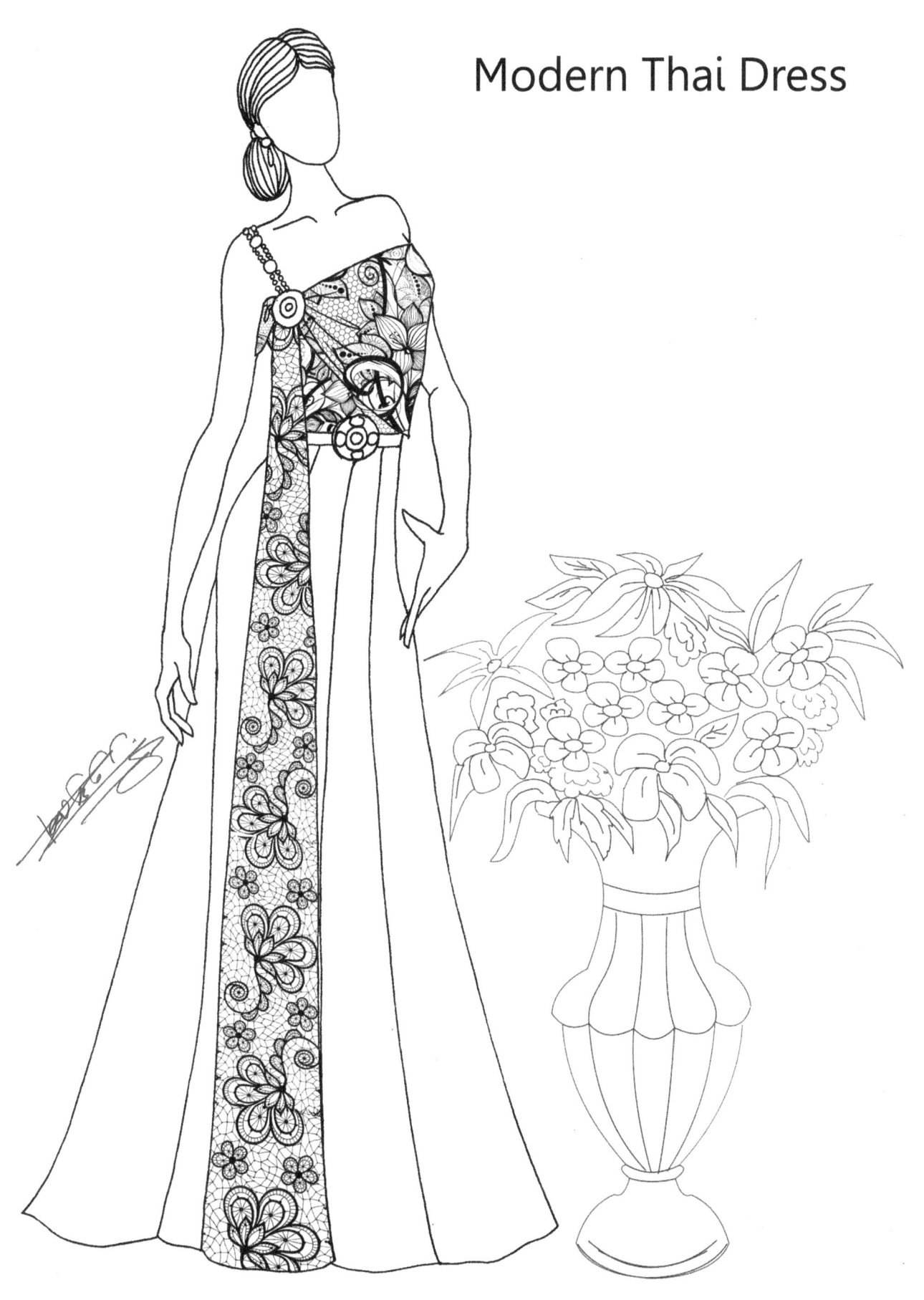

Thai Silk on Skirt

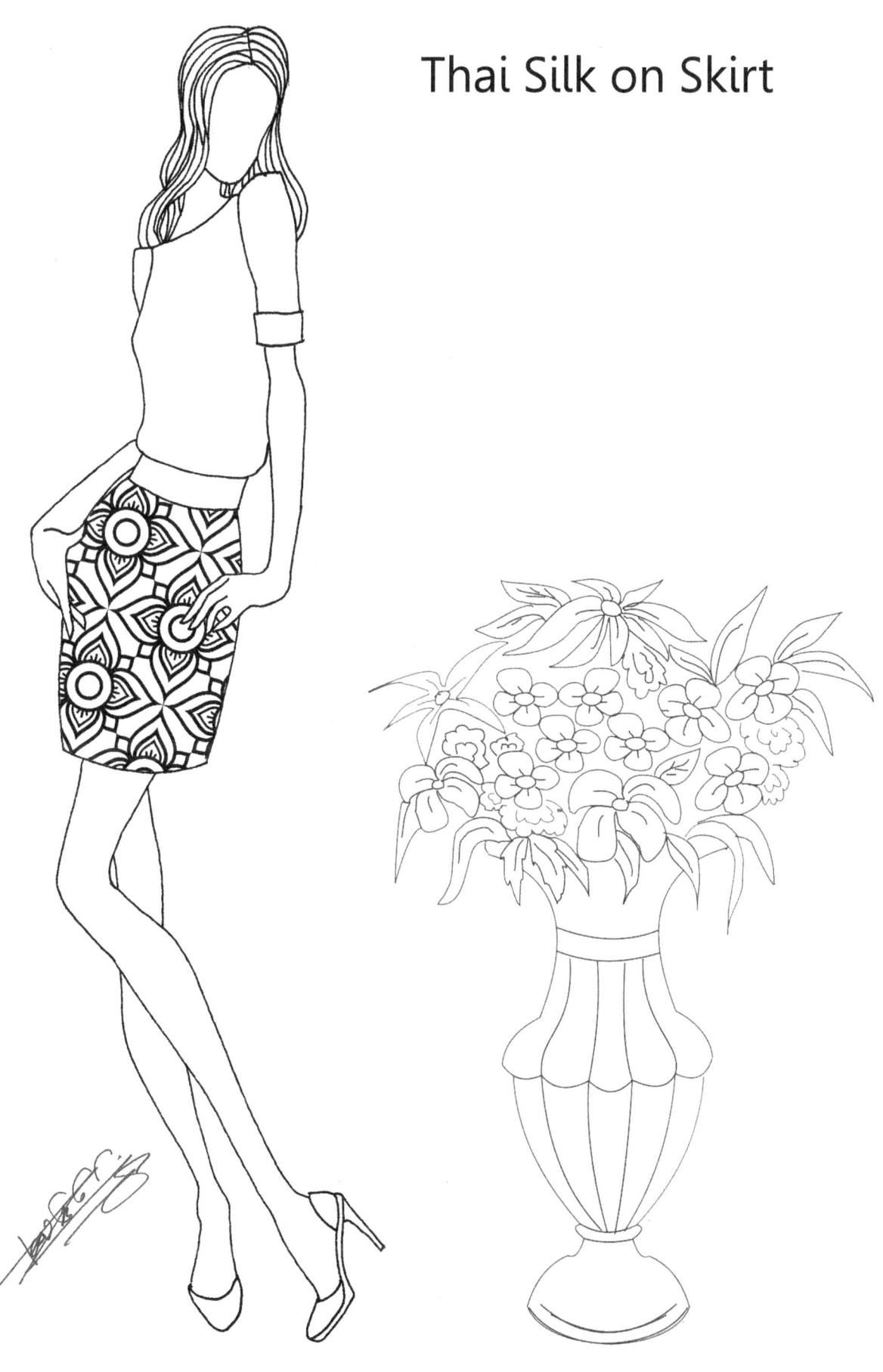

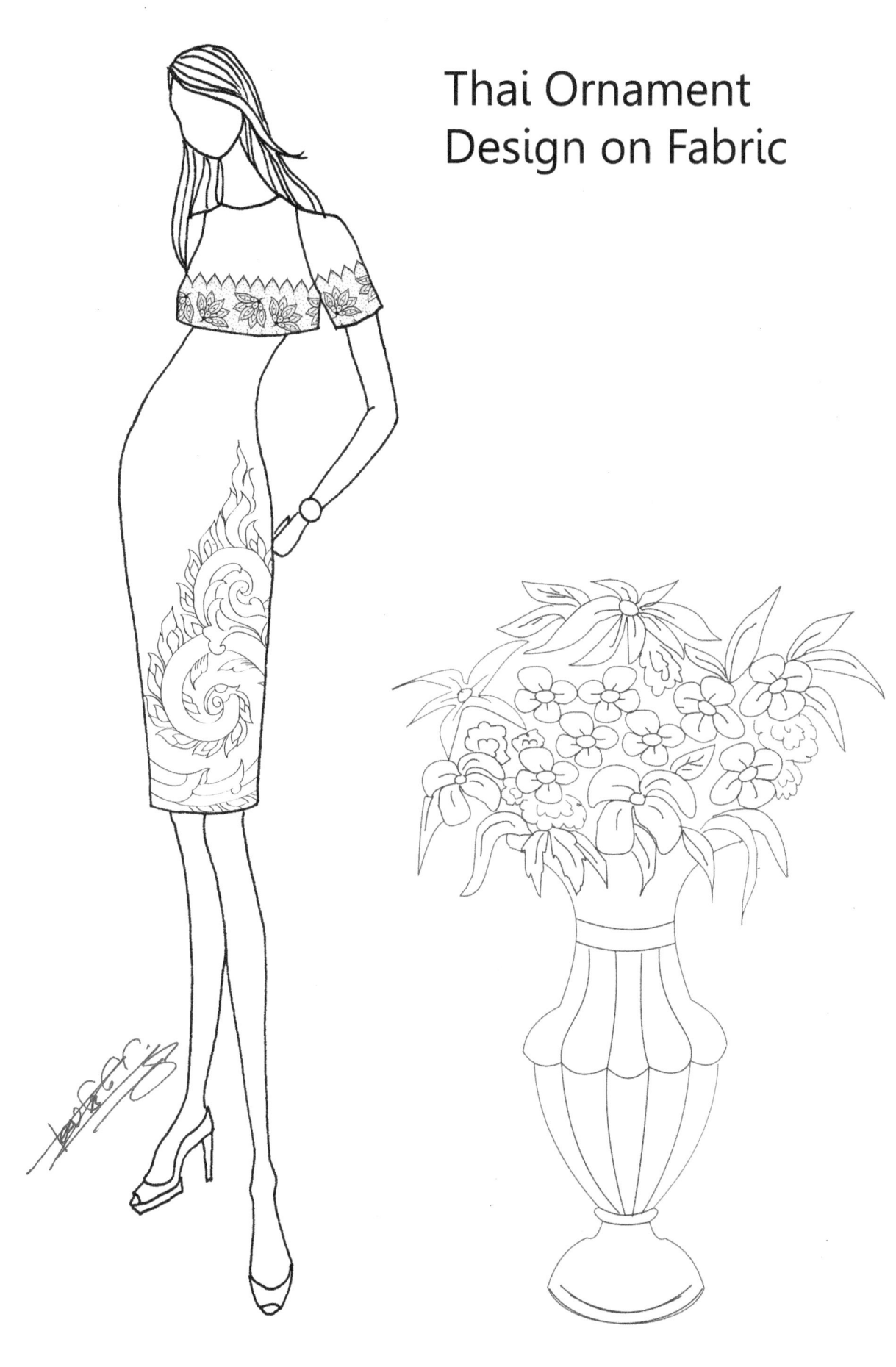

Thai Ornament Design on Fabric

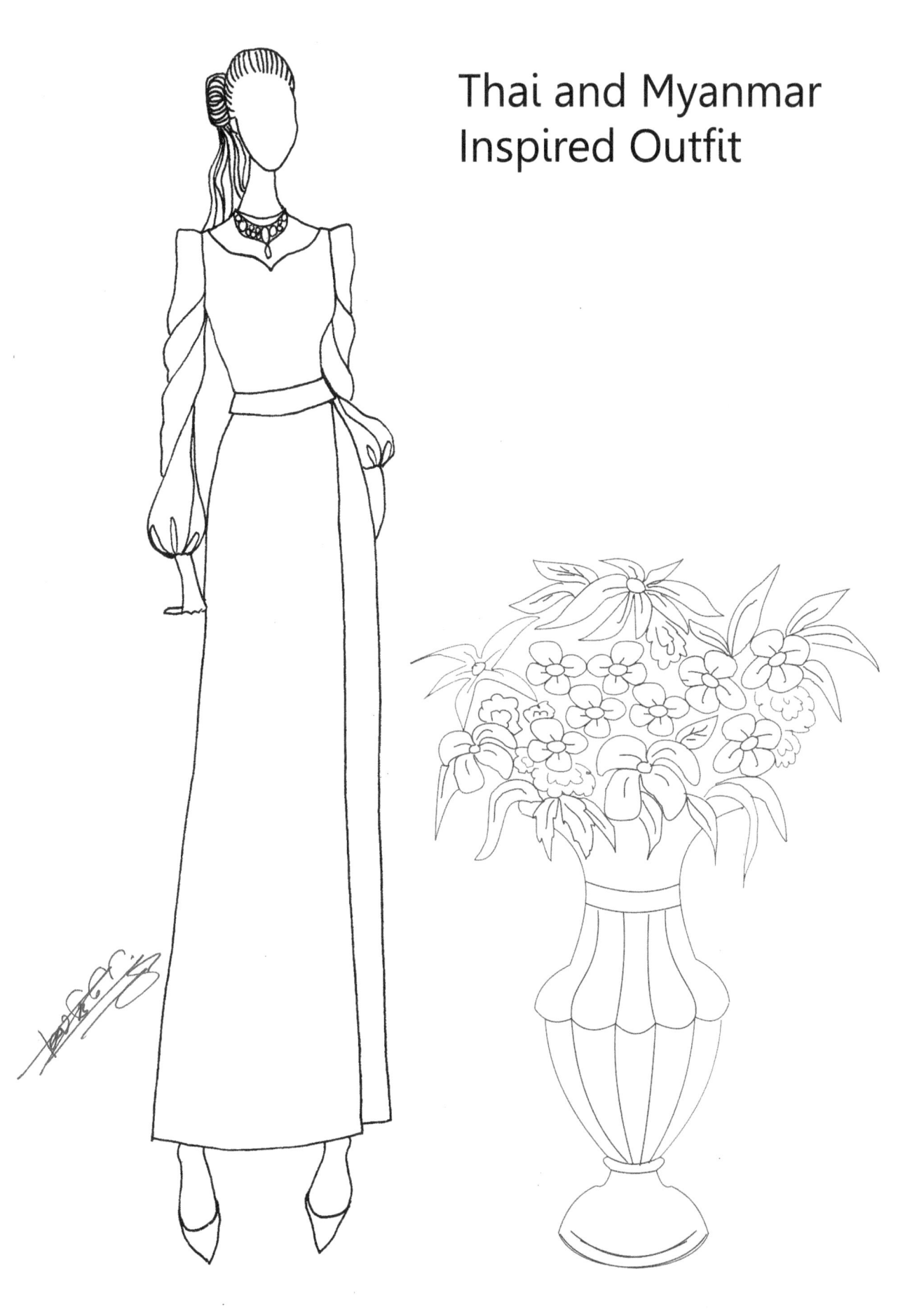

Thai and Myanmar Inspired Outfit